1757-1837

Witnesses
OF
MIRACLES
AND
MERCIES

1757-1837

Witnesses OF MIRACLES AND MERCIES

GLENN RAWSON AND DENNIS LYMAN

Background cover image: *First Vision* by Ken Corbett

Published by History of the Saints Inc., Sandy, Utah

Cover and interior design by Susan Lofgren

Copyright ©2020 History of the Saints, Dennis C. Lyman, Glenn Rawson

All rights reserved. No part of this book may be reproduced in any format or medium without the written permission of the publisher, History of the Saint's Inc. 1785 East Sunrise Park Drive, Sandy, Utah 84093. This work is not an official publication of The Church of Jesus Christ of Latter-day Saints. The views expressed within this work are the sole responsibility of the author and do not necessarily reflect the position of The Church of Jesus Christ of Latter-day Saints, or any other entity.

Printed in the United States of America
First Printing: September 2020

ISBN 978-0-9995327-8-2

Contents

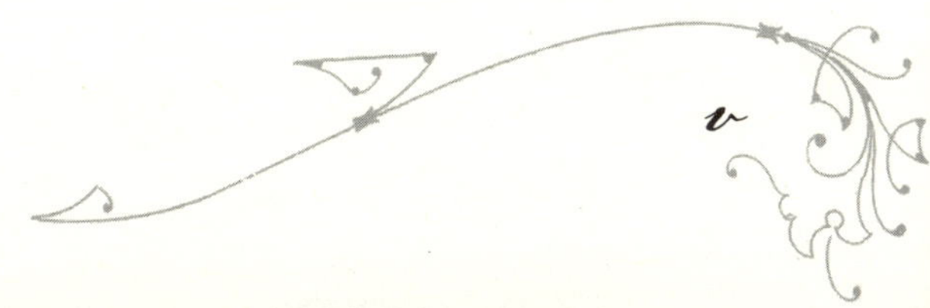

vi

Introduction

Beginning before the actual events of the Restoration, **Witnesses of Miracles and Mercies 1757–1837** moves forward chronologically. Each story is carefully researched and written according to the documents available, and each is the eyewitness account of someone who saw and knew for themselves the miracles and mercies of the Almighty.

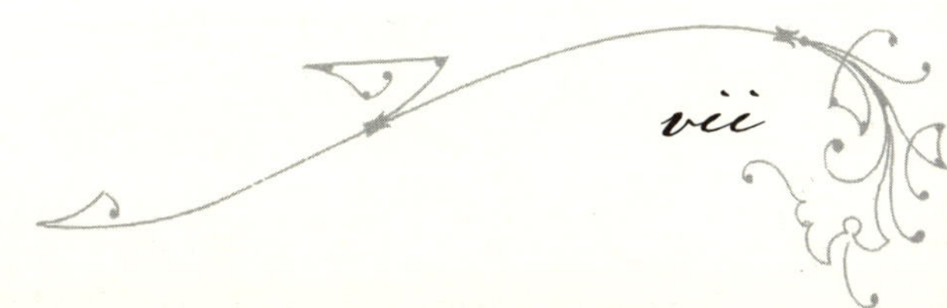

Farmer with Team of Oxen, by Otto von Thoren,
Wikimedia Commons

"Rush On, Brave Boys"

It was 1757 in Fort Edward, New York, and Solomon Mack—a young man in his early twenties who had enlisted in the French and Indian War two years earlier—now found himself driving ox teams in the service of the Crown. His teams had become lost, and he and a companion went over a dangerous trail through the forest in search of his valuable animals.

Suddenly Solomon found himself face to face with four armed and hostile Indians about 150 yards ahead. His traveling companion was 100 yards behind him. Alone, but not witless, Solomon cried out in a loud voice, "Rush on! Rush on! Brave boys, we'll have the devils! We'll have the devils!"

He later recorded what happened next: "I had no other weapon, only a staff; but I ran towards them, and the other man appearing in sight, gave them a terrible fright, and I saw them no more, but I am bound to say the grass did now grow under my feet."

Facing challenges head-on came to typify Solomon's approach to life. It was a legacy he would pass on to his family.

Seventy years later, late in the fall of 1827, Solomon's grandson—Joseph Smith Jr.—took a lesson from his revered grandfather. Joseph had just obtained the gold plates of the Book of Mormon from the angel Moroni, and mobs attempted every devisable stratagem to get the plates from him, but Joseph had been commanded of Moroni to use every effort to keep them safe.

Being warned that a mob might come, Joseph hid the plates beneath the hearth stones in the family home. No sooner were the hearth stones secured in place than a mob of armed men stormed up and surrounded the house. Thinking quickly, Joseph threw open the door of the house and, shouting as if he had an army at his command, ran from the house directly at the mob. Every man in the Smith home, including Joseph's fifteen-year-old brother Don Carlos, took up the act and charged out "with such fury upon the mob that it struck them with terror and dismay, and they fled before the little Spartan band into the woods." (See Lucy Mack Smith, *Biographical Sketches of Joseph Smith* [Liverpool, 1853], 108.)

The plates were safe once again.

Source: A Narrative of the Life of Solomon Mack, *olivercowdery.com*

Solomon Mack Sr., the son of Ebenezer Mack and
Hannah Hanlly, was born September 15, 1732, at Lyme,
New London County, Connecticut. A farmer, manufacturer,
merchant, shipmaster, real estate investor, and freighter, he
served in the French and Indian War from 1755–1759 and
in the American Revolutionary War in 1776. He married Lydia
Gates on January 4, 1759, in Lyme. Solomon moved to
Marlow, New Hampshire, in 1761 and to Gilsum, Cheshire
County, New Hampshire, by 1773. Solomon died on
August 23, 1820, and is buried in Bond Cemetery at Gilsum.

Source: Solomon Mack Sr., *josephsmithpapers.org*

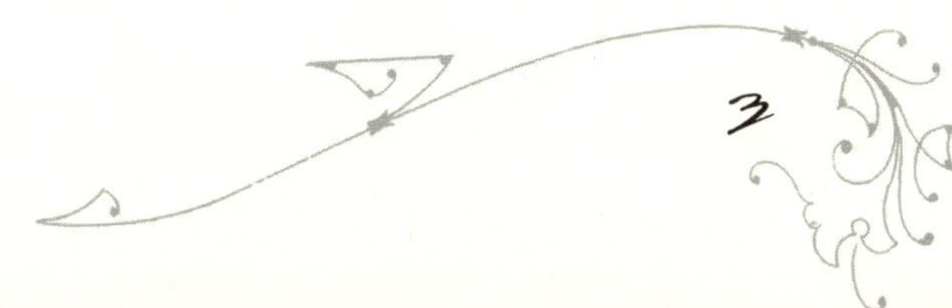

Lucy Mack Smith

A Mother's Covenant

 young mother lay deathly ill with a burning fever. It had begun as a heavy cold accompanied by a severe cough, and it had progressed from there. Every exertion was made to help her, and doctors came and ministered the best they could, but the final diagnosis was grim: tuberculosis. She was going to die.

During the sickness, her mother had attended to her with much anxiety, yet to no avail. She only grew weaker and weaker until even the slightest sound in the room was painful. In this agonizing condition, she began to contemplate her own death. *Was she ready to die?* Her answer was no. She did not know the ways of Christ, and there seemed to be a dark and lonesome chasm between her and the Almighty.

It was while she lay pondering these things that her husband entered the room where she lay. Taking her by the hand, he began to weep. "Oh, . . . my wife, my wife," he cried, "you must die. The doctors have all given you up and all say you cannot live."

As darkness fell over the room, her voice lifted to heaven, begging and pleading that she might be allowed to live to bring up her children and be a comfort to her husband. All through the night, her mind moved between heaven and earth. At one moment, she contemplated heaven and heavenly things; at the next, she returned to those she loved on earth—her babes and her companion.

Somewhere during that difficult night, her soul found resolve, and she entered into a covenant with the Almighty: if He would let her live, she would serve Him to the best of her abilities and would bring up her children in light and truth. Finally, there came a voice saying to her, "Seek, and ye shall find; knock and it shall be opened. Let your heart be comforted; ye believe in God, believe also in me."

Moments later her mother entered the room and exclaimed, "You are better!" As she turned to respond to her mother, she found the strength to speak for the first time in days. "Yes, Mother, the Lord will let me live, if I am faithful to the promise which I made to him to be a comfort to my mother, my husband, and my children."

From that point on she grew stronger until her body was well, but her soul was troubled, as she could find no one who could teach her with authority the ways of life and salvation. With steeled determination, she kept her promise to God and her family. And not only did she find the truth, but she raised an exceptional family that would change the world.

The year was 1802. The place was Randolph, Vermont. And
the tender, ailing young mother who entered that sacred covenant
was Lucy Mack Smith.

Source: Lucy Mack Smith, *History of Joseph Smith by His Mother* (Salt Lake
City: Stevens & Wallis, Inc., 1945), 33–35

Lucy Mack Smith, the daughter of Solomon Mack Sr.
and Lydia Gates, was born July 8, 1775, at Gilsum, Cheshire
County, New Hampshire. An oilcloth painter, nurse,
fund-raiser, and author, Lucy was baptized a member of
The Church of Jesus Christ of Latter-day Saints on April 6,
1830, most likely at Seneca Lake, Seneca County, New York.
Her husband, Joseph Smith Sr., died in 1840. Lucy joined
the Female Relief Society in March 1842 in Nauvoo. She
lived with her daughter Lucy Smith Millikin in Colchester,
McDonough County, Illinois, from 1846–1852. Lucy died at
Nauvoo on May 14, 1856. Her narrative history of the Smith
family, published as *Biographical Sketches of Joseph Smith* in
1853, has been an invaluable resource for the study of
Joseph Smith and the early Church.

Source: Lucy Mack Smith, *josephsmithpapers.org*

Sophronia Smith

"Your Child Is Dead"

There had been many reversals of the family fortunes, and just when circumstances were beginning to look brighter, a terrible epidemic swept the Connecticut River Valley in 1813.

Before it was over, some six thousand people lost their lives. It was typhoid fever.

Sophronia, only nine years old, was hit hard. The disease typically ran its course in three to four weeks, but Sophronia was attended by a physician for eighty-nine days. On the ninetieth day, the doctor concluded that she was too far gone to receive any benefit from the only medicine he knew to administer. With that, he gave her up.

The next night, Sophronia lay motionless on the bed, her eyes wide open, the look of death upon her countenance. Her mother stood looking at her, grieving. Just then her husband approached. They clasped hands and dropped to their knees before the bed in prayer. Together they poured out their souls to God, pleading with Him that He would spare their precious daughter a little longer.

God heard their prayers. Both mother and father were given by the Spirit to understand that their little girl would live—she would recover. However, when they arose from prayer, they found that Sophronia had stopped breathing. Her mother swiftly clutched a blanket, wrapped the child in it, swept her up into her arms, and began pacing the floor, holding the little girl close. There were those in the room who protested that her action was a waste of time. "It is all of no use," they said. "Your child is dead."

But the mother knew better.

One can only imagine the emotions in that room. Who would she trust—God and His whispered promises, or the resonant cries of the naysayers? The mother refused to let her go, refused to doubt.

"At length, [Sophronia] sobbed." Her mother continued to hold her close and pace the floor. Finally, the little girl sobbed again then looked up into her mother's face and began breathing normally.

It was enough. Sophronia would recover.

"My soul was satisfied," the faithful mother recorded, "but my strength was gone. I laid my daughter on the bed and sunk by her side, completely overpowered by the intensity of my feelings."

Sophronia Smith would make a full recovery, but that would not be the end of the family's trial. Shortly after that episode, Sophronia's younger brother, Joseph Smith Jr., would be struck down by the same disease. Before it was over, he would undergo a terrible ordeal that would nearly cost him his leg and his life.

It took a year, but finally the trial was over for the Smith family. Mother Smith said, "Indeed, we felt to acknowledge the hand of God, more in preserving our lives through such a tremendous scene of affliction, than if we had . . . seen nothing but health and prosperity."

Sources: Lucy Mack Smith, *History of Joseph Smith by His Mother* (Salt Lake City: Stevens & Wallis, Inc., 1945), 52–53

Lucy Mack Smith, History, 1845, page 57, *josephsmithpapers.org*

Sophronia Smith, the daughter of Joseph Smith Sr. and Lucy Mack, was born Mary 16, 1803, at Tunbridge, Orange County, Vermont. Sophronia married Calvin W. Stoddard on December 30, 1827, at Palmyra, Wayne County, New York. She lived at Macedon, Wayne County, in 1830 and was baptized a member of The Church of Jesus Christ of Latter-day Saints, possibly that same year. Sophronia migrated to Kirtland, Geauga County, Ohio, with the Lucy Mack Smith company. Her husband died in 1836, and she married William McCleary on February 11, 1838, in Kirtland. She was received into the Reorganized Church of Jesus Christ of Latter Day Saints on April 8, 1873, based on her original baptism. Sophronia died on July 22, 1876, at Fountain Green, Hancock County, Illinois.

Source: Sophronia Smith McCleary, *josephsmithpapers.org*

Mount Tambora

Sumbawa, Indonesia

Mount Tambora and the Year Without a Summer

On April 10, 1815, Mount Tambora on the island of Sumbawa in the Indonesian Archipelago erupted, explosively ejecting some thirty-eight cubic miles of material twenty-seven miles into the stratosphere. The eruption was so devastating that it blacked out the sun for two days at a distance of 370 miles.

Tambora was the largest volcanic eruption in recorded history. The explosion blew more than 4,700 feet of the mountain off the top, and it left a crater more than four miles across. The explosion was heard 1,600 miles away.

The pyroclastic flow spread twelve miles in all directions and buried the village of Tambora, freezing in time all its inhabitants beneath ten feet of volcanic rubble. Tsunamis caused by the volcano reached a height of thirteen feet and slammed into the surrounding islands, killing thousands. In all, it is estimated that Mount Tambora killed 71,000 people. An estimated 12,000 were killed directly by the eruption.

Explosions and aftershocks continued for years afterward. High-altitude ash was carried on the prevailing winds around the globe, causing varied optical phenomenon, including prolonged and brilliant sunsets, stunning twilights, sunspots, and red fog.

In the aftermath, the summer of 1816 became the year without a summer. The ash circled the earth, filtering the sun's rays. As a result, the northeastern United States was gripped by a killer frost on June 4, 1816. Snow fell up to a foot in some places. The terrible cold lasted throughout the summer and ruined most agricultural crops. The 1810s became the coldest decade on record.

When all was considered, Tambora disrupted the lives of millions around the globe, destroying crops, intensifying diseases, causing famines, triggering riots, and resulting in countless deaths.

Among those families whose lives and livelihood were shattered by a lone mountain across the world was a rural farm family in Vermont. Three times that summer the farmer planted his crops, and three times they failed. He was ruined. Losing his own prosperous farm, the family patriarch was reduced to being a tenant farmer.

He had had enough of the rugged mountains of Vermont, and he decided to seek his fortune in newly opened land to the south and west. Accordingly, he moved his family to a new settlement called Palmyra in the State of New York. By so doing, he brought his young son, Joseph Smith Jr., to live near a hill that would come to be called Cumorah, where Joseph would one day unearth a sacred record that we know as the Book of Mormon.

Sources: Mount Tambora, Volcano, Indonesia, *britannica.com*

1815 Eruption of Mount Tambora, *en.wikipedia.org*

"Left to Wallow in Blood until a Stranger Picked Me Up"

It had been a devastating experience, that summer of 1816 in Norwich, Vermont. Three times that year Joseph Smith Sr. had planted his crops; three times those crops had been nipped by frost and destroyed. He was through with Vermont.

As he meditated on his plight, he declared that he intended to arrange his business affairs and go to New York, where wheat grew in abundance. He was reluctant to leave his family, but Lucy assured him that if he went ahead to get things ready, she could make the journey with the children.

Sometime that year, Father Smith set out with a friend named Howard for a new community in upstate New York called Palmyra. There he went to work and prepared to send for his family. He rented a small home on west Main Street, just where Stafford Road intersected it, and sent for his family.

After settling the last-minute demands of creditors, Lucy rode by sleigh to Royalton, where she bid her mother a final tearful farewell—never to see her again in this life. From there she and the children loaded into a wagon driven by a man named Caleb Howard, and they began the three-hundred-mile journey to Palmyra.

Howard would prove less than friendly. As one example, he forced Joseph, then only eleven years old, to walk. In addition to

15

his being a child, Joseph was still recovering from a serious leg operation, and walking was difficult and painful. When Alvin and Hyrum protested that Joseph should not be forced to walk, Howard knocked them down with the butt of his whip.

It didn't end there. Just a few miles west of Utica, New York, knowing that Lucy was out of money, Howard threw their goods into the street and attempted to steal their wagon. Lucy ran out, grabbed the reins of the team, and in a loud voice announced to bystanders that she was being robbed. Now with an audience, Lucy declared, "As for you, sir, I have no use for you, and you can ride or walk the rest of the way as you please, but I shall take charge of my own affairs."

With that, Lucy and her children set out once more. Joseph was assigned to ride with another family that was making the same journey, but one of their older sons knocked Joseph out of the sleigh; they rode off without him. Joseph said he was "left to wallow in my blood until a stranger came along, picked me up, and carried me to the town of Palmyra."

Finally, the Smith family reached Palmyra in January 1817. Lucy records, "The joy I felt in throwing myself and my children upon the care and affection of a tender husband and father doubly paid me for all I had suffered. The children surrounded their father clinging to his neck, covering his face with tears and kisses that were heartily reciprocated by him."

And with that, the Smith family made their home in Palmyra, New York, the place where the Lord had directed that the Restoration begin.

Source: Lucy Mack Smith, *History*, 1844–1845, page 6, bk. 3, *josephsmithpapers.org*

If Any of You Lack Wisdom . . .

J oseph Smith was about twelve years of age when he became "seriously impressed with the all important concerns for the immortal soul." He "felt to mourn for [his] own sins" and "cried unto the Lord for mercy; considering it of first importance that [he] should be right in matters that involve eternal consequence." He attended the "several meetings" of the churches in his area, "as often as occasion would permit." He wanted to know which church was true.

"I knew not who was right," he said, "I found that there was a great clash in religious sentiment; if I went to one society they referred me to one plan, and another to another, each one pointing to his own particular creed as the summum bonum of perfection."

"In the midst of this war of words and tumult of opinions, [Joseph] often said to himself, what is to be done? Who of all these parties are right…and how shall I know it?" This led him to "searching the scriptures, believing . . . that they contained the word of God."

One day he read in the book of James, "If any of you lack wisdom, let him ask of God, that giveth to all men liberally, and upbraideth not; and it shall be given him" (James 1:5).

"Never" Joseph wrote, "did any passage of scripture come with more power to the heart of man than this did at this time to mine. . . . At length I came to the conclusion that I must either remain in darkness and confusion or else I must do as James directs."

Joseph determined that he would, in fact, ask God. "I immediately went out into the woods," he said, "where my father had a clearing, and went to the stump where I had struck my axe. . . . I kneeled down and prayed."

No sooner had he done so that he was seized upon by some unseen power that completely overcame him. His mind was filled with darkness, doubt, and all manner of evil. The force was not an "imaginary ruin but . . . some actual being from the unseen world" that nearly killed him.

Joseph exerted all his powers to call upon God, and then discovered a light exactly over his head, brighter than the sun at noonday. He called it "a pillar of fire." The light descended gradually and "increased in brightness and magnitude, so that, by the time that it reached the tops of the trees, the whole wilderness, for some distance around was illuminated in a most glorious and brilliant manner."

The light "produced a peculiar sensation throughout his whole system." Joseph was "filled with the Spirit of God." "I saw two personages," he recorded, first one then the other, "whose brightness and glory defy all description, standing above me in the air." They "exactly resembled each other in features and likeness.

First Vision, by Jon McNaughton

"One of them spake unto me," he said, "calling me by name and said, pointing to the other— 'This is my beloved son. Hear him!'"

Joseph later described that the personage was of a "light complexion, blue eyes, [with] a piece of white cloth drawn over his shoulders."

"Joseph, my son," the Lord said, "Thy sins are forgiven thee. Go thy way. Walk in my statutes and keep my commandments."

Joseph recorded, "No sooner did I get possession of myself so as to be able to speak, than I asked the Personages who stood above me in the light, which of all the sects was right. I was answered that I must join none of them." "I was expressly commanded 'to go not after them' at the same time receiving a promise that the fullness of the Gospel should at some future time be made known unto me." Joseph saw "many angels in this vision," and Joseph was told "many other things" that he did not write.

Following one of the greatest visions in all of recorded history, "Joseph rejoiced with great joy for the Lord was with him [for many days]." His soul was "filled with love," he wrote, but then added, "But [I] could find none that would believe the heavenly vision."

Source: Primary Accounts of Joseph Smith's First Vision of Deity, *josephsmithpapers.org*

He Carried Me Home

It was the time of year to harvest the corn. All the community turned to their fields; men and boys hired, helped, and shared, vowing to stay with the task until the entire crop was secured for the winter.

In one field, a man named Palmer sent his sons out to work. One afternoon, their six-year-old sister tagged along with them. While the men worked, the little girl occupied herself by playing among the corn rows until the day's end.

When evening came and the work day ended, the boys prepared to leave the field.

By this time, the little one had worn herself out and was too tired to walk all the way home. She asked her brothers to carry her. When they refused, she started to cry. Hearing her, one of her father's hired hands walked over, picked her up, and placed her on his shoulders. She threw her arm around his neck and, with his arm thrown across her feet to steady her, he carried her all the way home.

That act of gentle kindness stayed with that little girl for the rest of her life. And while so many of that community and country would turn against that young man, including her own family, she carried that simple memory all her life. The young, kind-hearted farm hand who left such a lasting impression was Joseph Smith Jr.

Source: Hyrum and Helen Mae Andrus, *They Knew the Prophet* (Salt Lake: Deseret Book, 1999), 1–2

At Cumorah

God does much of his work through mortal men, and sometimes so much depends on those men.

Monday morning, September 22, 1823, seventeen-year-old Joseph Smith Jr. climbed up the forested west face of a hill later to be called Cumorah. The previous night, Joseph had been visited by an angel, who had told him of an ancient record buried in that hill. The angel Moroni showed him by vision the exact place where the record was buried. Joseph now stood before a large stone that he knew covered that record.

The stone was too heavy to lift, so Joseph found a lever and "with a little exertion raised it up" (Joseph Smith—History 1:52). Under the stone was a box formed of stones and mortared together with cement. Inside the box was an ancient record written on gold plates giving an account of the former inhabitants of the Americas.

"On attempting to take possession of the record a shock was produced upon his system, by an invisible power which deprived him, in a measure, of his natural strength. He . . . made another attempt, but was more sensibly shocked than before." Calculating

23

that he needed to try harder, he reached again "when his strength failed him more than at either of the former times . . . he exclaimed, 'Why can I not obtain this book?' From nearby came a voice, 'Because you have not kept the commandments of the Lord'" (*Messenger and Advocate,* 2:198). It was the angel of the Lord.

Joseph had been warned that he must have no other object in view in getting the plates but to glorify God (see Joseph Smith—History 1:46). He realized that in his thoughts he had been "tempted of the adversary and sought the plates to obtain riches" (Joseph Smith 1832 History).

Humbled, Joseph prayed.

> The heavens were opened and the glory of the Lord shone round about, and rested upon him. While he thus stood gazing and admiring, the angel said, 'Look!' and as he thus spake he beheld the prince of darkness, surrounded by his innumerable train of associates. All this passed before him, and the heavenly messenger said, 'All this is shown, the good and the evil, the holy and impure, the glory of God and the power of darkness, that you may know hereafter the two powers and never be influenced or overcome by that wicked one.' (*Messenger and Advocate,* 2:198)

One year later, on September 22, 1824, "Joseph again visited the place where he found the plates the year previous. . . . He fully expected to carry them home with him." He removed the plates from the box, and then thinking there might be something else in the box of monetary value, he set the plates down, turned back, and carefully covered the box again. "He turned [around] to take the Record again, but . . . it was gone. . . . He was much alarmed. He kneeled down and asked the Lord why the Record had been taken from him." Once again, the angel appeared and reminded him that "he had been commanded not to lay the plates down" (Lucy Mack Smith, *History of Joseph Smith,* 95).

He was permitted to open the box again. Upon seeing the plates once more inside the box, he reached for them, but "was hurled back upon the ground with great violence." Joseph returned home, weeping with disappointment, "aware that [his family] would expect him to bring the plates home with him" (*History of Joseph Smith*, 83–84).

The commandments of God are strict. It is not enough for any of us to be merely *willing* to keep the commandments of God. We must practice obedience until, by the grace of God, we are obedient.

On September 22, 1825, after another year had passed, Joseph returned again to the hill. We have no account of what happened at that time.

In September 1826, Joseph returned to the hill and met the angel. Joseph asked for the record but was told that this was not the year. The angel told him, "If he would do right according to the will of God he might obtain it on the 22nd of September next, and if not he never would have them." The angel also added that he "might have the book if he brought with him the right person." When Joseph asked who that "right person" was, he was told that he would know. That person was later revealed to be Emma Hale (*Joseph Knight Sr. Recollection*).

25

Just after midnight on September 22, 1827, Joseph and Emma Smith, now married, returned to the hill. Emma stayed with the carriage while Joseph climbed the hill and took up the record.

The angel of the Lord stood by and said, Now
you have got the record into your own hands, and
you are but a man, therefore you will have to be
watchful and faithful to your trust, or you will
be overpowered by wicked men. . . . Beware, and
look well to your ways, and you shall have power
to retain it, until the time for it to be translated.
(*Lucy Mack Smith History*)

Sources: *Latter Day Saints' Messenger and Advocate,* No. 6, *archive.org*
History, circa Summer 1832, page 5, *josephsmithpapers.org*
Joseph Knight's Recollection of Early Mormon History, *boap.org*
Lucy Mack Smith, *History,* 1845, page 88, *josephsmithpapers.org*

The First Real Sacrifice in Faith

When we speak of faith and courage, the story of a young woman's decision to wed should ever be remembered.

On January 18, 1827, Emma Hale, then twenty-two years old, traveled north up the Susquehanna River from her home in Harmony, Pennsylvania, to visit her sister, who was living near Colesville, New York. While there, Emma and Joseph Smith Jr. discussed marriage—and not for the first time.

Emma and Joseph had known each other since the fall of 1825, when Joseph had lived with Emma's family while working in the area. The two became attracted to each other, and perhaps with good reason. Joseph was taller than the average men of his day, around six feet; he was also powerfully built, with light brown hair and clean-cut features. He was frequently described as a handsome young man.

Emma too was tall—about five-foot-nine, well figured, with long dark hair, dark eyes, and an olive complexion. George A. Smith later described her as the "most beautiful woman in the universe"—a sentiment echoed by others.

Emma and Joseph courted according to the social customs of the day, attending dances, participating in corn-huskings, and writing letters. In time they came to agree that they wanted to be married. Complying with social custom, though it was not required, Joseph asked Emma's father, Isaac Hale, if they could be wed. Isaac's answer was no. He did not approve, and he forbade it.

Consider how difficult this must have been for Emma. She and her father were particularly close. The records seem to indicate that Emma was a favorite of her father, and he was especially fond of her. If she married Joseph, she would be sacrificing any relationship with her father and her family. There would be no cherished wedding in the family parlor with her friends and bridesmaids where all the family gathered in celebration. Moreover, she would be giving up her home, all her friends, the substantial dowry she had accumulated, and the comfortable, relatively affluent lifestyle that her father had provided. She had a choice: she could keep all she had ever known and loved, or she could marry Joseph.

And what came with Joseph? Emma was well-educated and cultured for the time; Joseph, on the other hand, was a rough-hewn frontiersman, mostly illiterate—and while he was studying hard to change that, Emma said, he still could not craft a well-worded letter. That's not all. He was a hated and a hunted man. Twice already he had been arrested and put on trial, and while that represented perhaps the worst of the persecution, there were those who had threatened his life and despised him for what he believed: that he had seen God and Christ, that an angel was his mentor and tutor, that the heavens had been opened to him, and that not many months hence and the Book of Mormon would be brought forth through him. Simply put, Joseph was not a popular man. If Emma chose Joseph, she would take his part. Whatever came upon him by the will of God and the wickedness of men would be hers as well.

Emma made her choice. On January 18, 1827, Emma married Joseph at the home of Zachariah Tarbell in South Bainbridge, New York. Whoever else may have been attendance that night, it was not Emma's family.

Emma's decision to marry Joseph represents the first real sacrifice in faith for the restored gospel in this last dispensation. To marry Joseph was to give up everything and proclaim that he was telling the truth. On that day she took his part and carried it all the days of her life.

If ever there lived a person who knew Joseph, who suffered immeasurably because of him and what he taught, who could have exposed him if he were a fraud—that person would have been Emma. But she never did. She who knew him best bore the strongest witness that he was a true prophet.

Source: History of the Saints Interview with Mark Lyman Staker, December 2013

Emma Hale Smith, the daughter of Isaac Hale and Elizabeth Lewis, was born July 10, 1804, at Willingborough Township (later known as Harmony), Susquehanna County, Pennsylvania. A scribe, editor, boardinghouse operator, and clothier, she was a member of the Methodist Church

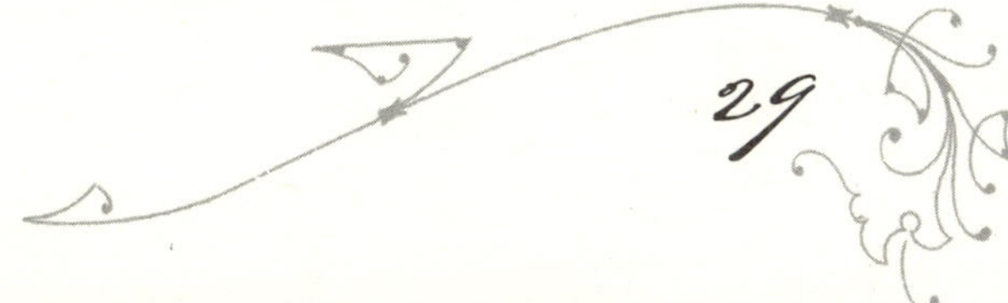

Emma Smith, by Lee Greene Richards

at Harmony (and later in Oakland). She was married to Joseph Smith on January 18, 1827, at South Bainbridge (later Afton), Chenango County, New York; Zachariah Tarbell performed the ceremony. Emma assisted Joseph Smith as scribe during translation of the Book of Mormon at Harmony in 1828; she joined him during completion of the translation at the Peter Whitmer Sr. farm in Fayette, Seneca County, New York, in the summer of 1829. She was baptized a member of The Church of Jesus Christ of Latter-day Saints by Oliver Cowdery on June 28, 1830, at Colesville, Broome County, New York. Emma was appointed president of the Female Relief Society of Nauvoo on March 17, 1842. Emma's husband was murdered June 27, 1844; she fled to Fulton, Fulton County, Illinois, in September 1846 and lived there until February 1847, when she returned to Nauvoo. Emma married her second husband, Lewis Crum Bidamon, on December 23, 1847, at Nauvoo. She affiliated with the Reorganized Church of Jesus Christ of Latter Day Saints in 1860. Emma died at Nauvoo on April 30, 1879.

Source: Emma Hale Smith, *josephsmithpapers.org*

The Battle Has Begun

The mind and heart of God are not the mind and heart of men, and what is worthy of remembering in the eyes of God is often trivial and of no consequence to men. In that light, we'd like to remember a monumental moment in the eternal affairs of this earth and dedicate that effort to those modern warriors of light anxiously engaged in the cause of Christ.

Late one fall evening after Heber and Vilate Kimball had retired to their bed, they were awakened suddenly by a sharp knocking at their door. A neighbor, John Greene, stood at the door and bade them come out and see the incredible scenery in the heavens. They did so, and it was a beautiful starlit New England night, so exceptionally clear and brilliant that Heber said later he could have seen clearly enough to pick up a pin.

As the little group watched, a white smoke or cloud formed on the eastern horizon and slowly began to rise upward. As it did so, it formed itself into a belt spreading across the sky toward the southwest accompanied by the sound of a rushing mighty wind.

Gradually, that belt flattened out and broadened into a bow like a rainbow, becoming transparent with a bluish cast, stretching from one horizon to the other.

No sooner had the bow formed than an army of men appeared arising from the east and began marching twelve abreast across the bow toward the west. As vivid and real as men in the flesh, they marched in the most profound order, every man stepping in the tracks of his leader in perfect synchronization. They were dressed in the full battle gear of nineteenth-century soldiers, carrying muskets fitted with bayonets. They were so clear and distinct that Heber and the small group of neighbors could distinguish the features of their faces and hear the jingle of their equipment as they moved.

Shortly, the entire bow from horizon to horizon was crowded and filled with marching men. The sound of that marching reached the ears of the astonished onlookers with clarity.

Heber later described the event this way: "No man could judge of my feelings when I beheld that army of men, as plainly as ever I saw armies of men in the flesh; it seemed as though [the very] hair of my head was alive."

When the celestial army reached the western horizon, it was met by an opposing force, and a battle ensued. The noise of the rush of men and the clash of arms was distinct and unmistakable. Heber and his friends looked upon this scene for hours, until finally it gradually disappeared.

Heber's wife, somewhat afraid, turned to one of the older men in the group and asked, "Father Young, what does all this mean?"

"Why, it's one of the signs of the coming of the Son of Man," he replied.

And indeed it was, even though the world missed it, just as surely as the meridian world missed the birth of Christ. For that momentous night marked the commencement of the marvelous work and wonder spoken of by Isaiah—that oh, so significant night. It was the night of September 22, 1827. Just a few miles away on that same night, the Prophet Joseph Smith was receiving the gold plates from the angel Moroni.

The battle had begun.

Source: Adapted from Orson F. Whitney, *Life of Heber C. Kimball: An Apostle—The Father and Founder of the British Mission,* 2nd ed. (Salt Lake City: Bookcraft, 1945), 16–17

Heber C. Kimball, the son of Solomon Farnham Kimball and Anna Spaulding, was born June 14, 1801, in Sheldon, Franklin County, Vermont. A blacksmith and potter, he married Vilate Murray on November 22, 1822, in Mendon, Monroe

County, New York. Heber was a member of the Baptist Church in Mendon in 1831, and was baptized a member of The Church of Jesus Christ of Latter-day Saints by Alpheus Gifford on April 15, 1832, at Mendon. Heber presided over the first Latter-day Saint missionaries sent to Great Britain in 1837–1838. He moved to Far West, Caldwell County, Missouri, in 1838; there he worked closely with Brigham Young and others in supervising the removal of Latter-day Saints from Missouri in 1838–1839. A member of the Brigham Young vanguard pioneer company, Heber arrived in the Salt Lake Valley in July 1847. He was sustained as first counselor to Brigham Young in the First Presidency on December 27, 1847, at what became Council Bluffs, Pottawattamie County, Iowa. Elected the lieutenant governor in the provisional State of Deseret, Heber also served in the Utah territorial legislature. He died June 22, 1868, at Salt Lake City.

Source: Heber Chase Kimball, *josephsmithpapers.org*

"A Shock of the Power of God"

Born in Connecticut, Solomon Chamberlain suffered the death of his father when he was only eight years old. Solomon said of the years following that experience:

> From the time my father died, till I was 19 years of age I lived a very wicked life. About that time, I had a vision of hell, and which alarmed me very much, and I reformed. . . . My visions so alarmed me, I was in sorrow and repentance for many days, on account of my sins, I thought I would give all the world if I could find a man that could tell me what I should do to be saved. I sought much, but could find none.

Solomon pleaded in prayer night and day until finally the word of the Lord came to him, saying, "Solomon, thy sins are forgiven thee. Go in peace and sin no more."

In about the year 1816, Solomon received another vision in which he was told there was no true Church on the earth, but that the true faith with prophets and Apostles would soon be restored. He was also told that another book like unto the Bible would come forth.

Years passed, and Solomon grew restless. Then one day he had occasion to travel to upper Canada. He boarded a canal boat and traveled west along the Erie Canal. As he passed the village of Palmyra, Solomon felt strangely impressed to get off the boat. He did. Then came another impression to journey south, which he did. He lodged for the night there with some local residents.

The next morning the lady of the house asked him if he had heard of the gold Bible.

"When she mentioned Gold Bible," Solomon recorded, "I felt a shock of the power of God go from head to foot. I said to myself, 'I shall soon find why I have been led in this singular manner.'"

At that moment, Solomon was only half a mile from the Smith farm. He went there. As he entered the home, he asked, "Is there anyone here that believes in visions or revelations?"

Can you imagine Hyrum's surprise when he heard the stranger's question? Upon learning they were a visionary household, Solomon expounded his views of a future Restoration of Christ's Church. The Smiths were astonished.

Solomon spent two days with the Smith family while they taught him. Then Hyrum and Solomon went into Palmyra and visited the Grandin Print Shop, where the printing of the Book of Mormon had just begun. When the proof sheets containing the first sixty-four pages of the Book of Mormon came off Grandin's press, Solomon was so excited that he asked for permission to take some. He was given permission.

Sheets in hand, Solomon went on his way to Canada, preaching the Book of Mormon before it was even printed. He raised the warning voice telling people to prepare for the great work of God that was coming. Among those who heard him were Phineas and Brigham Young.

When the Church was organized, Solomon was there. From that day forward, wherever the Church went, Solomon went, suffering everything but death while he served faithfully and followed the prophets all the way to Utah. Solomon died in 1862—his last days spent, he said, "endeavoring to live every day in a way that I am willing to meet the Judge of all the earth at any time."

Source: Solomon Chamberlain, 1788–1862, *boap.org*

Solomon Chamberlain, born July 30, 1788, holds notoriety in the early Latter-day Saint movement for being the first to evangelize the printed Book of Mormon. He preached from proof sheets during a tour among Baptists and Reformed Methodists in New York and Upper Canada while the Grandin Print Shop in Palmyra, New York, prepared volumes for publication. Solomon made two trips to the Salt Lake Valley, the first in 1847 with Brigham Young's vanguard company, in which he was part of the 11th Company of Ten led by John S. Higbee. He then returned to Winter Quarters after only a month in the valley to collect his family. Solomon died in 1862.

Sources: Solomon Chamberlain, *en.wikipedia.org*

Solomon Chamberlain, Pioneer Overland Travel, *history.churchofjesuschrist.org*

37

Lithograph by C.C.A. Christensen, 1886,
Library of Congress

Courage in Defending the Book of Mormon

While the Book of Mormon was being printed, Oliver Cowdery overheard a group of Palmyra residents plotting and scheming against the book. Their plan was to snatch it away from Mother Smith and burn it. Meaning to follow through with their plan, they came to the house and asked her to read the manuscript to them. The following is her account of those events:

> "Mrs. Smith, we hear that you have a gold bible; we have come to see if you will be so kind as to show it to us?"
>
> "No, gentlemen," said I, "we have no gold bible, but we have a translation of some gold plates, which have been brought forth for the purpose of making known to the world the plainness of the gospel, and also to give a history of the people which formerly inhabited this continent." I then proceeded to relate the substance of what is contained in the Book of Mormon, dwelling

particularly upon the principles of religion therein contained. I endeavored to show them the similarity between these principles, and the simplicity of the gospel taught by Jesus Christ in the New Testament.

"Notwithstanding all this," said I, "the different denominations are very much opposed to us. The Universalists are alarmed lest their religion should suffer loss, the Presbyterians tremble for their salaries, the Methodists also come, and they rage, for they worship a God without body or parts, and they know that our faith comes in contact with this principle."

After hearing me through, the gentlemen said, "Can we see the manuscript, then?"

"No, sir," replied I, "you cannot see it. I have told you what it contains, and that must suffice."

He made no reply to this, but said, "Mrs. Smith, you and the most of your children have belonged to our church for some length of time, and we respect you very highly. You say a good deal about the Book of Mormon, which your son has found, and you believe much of what he tells you, yet we cannot bear the thoughts of losing you, and they do wish—I wish, that if you do believe those things, you would not say anything more upon the subject—I do wish you would not."

"Deacon Beckwith," said I, "if you should stick my flesh full of faggots, and even burn me at the stake, I would declare, as long as God should give me breath, that Joseph has got that Record, and that I know it to be true."

At this, he observed to his companions, "You see it is of no use to say anything more to her, for we cannot change her mind." Then, turning to me, he said, "Mrs. Smith, I see that it is not possible to persuade you out of your belief, therefore I deem it unnecessary to say anything more upon the subject."

"No, sir," said I, "it is not worth your while."

He then bade me farewell, and went out to see Hyrum, when the following conversation took place between them:

Deacon Beckwith: "Mr. Smith, do you not think that you may be deceived about that Record, which your brother pretends to have found?"

Hyrum: "No, sir, I do not."

Deacon Beckwith: "Well, now, Mr. Smith, if you find that you are deceived, and that he has not got the Record, will you confess the fact to me?"

Hyrum: "Will you, Deacon Beckwith, take one of the books, when they are printed, and read it, asking God to give you an evidence that you may know whether it is true?"

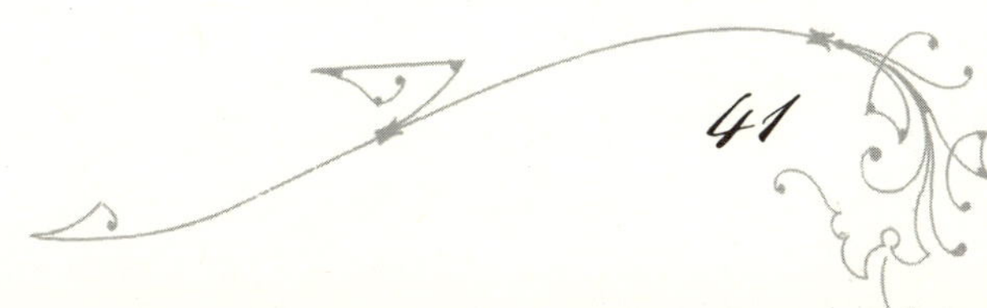

41

Deacon Beckwith: "I think it beneath me to take so much trouble, however, if you will promise that you will confess to me that Joseph never had the plates, I will ask for a witness whether the book is true."

Hyrum: "I will tell you what I will do, Mr. Beckwith, if you do get a testimony from God, that the book is not true, I will confess to you that it is not true."

Upon this they parted, and the Deacon next went to Samuel, who quoted to him, Isaiah 56: 9–11: "All ye beasts of the field, come to devour; yea, all ye beasts in the forest. His watchmen are blind: they are all ignorant, they are all dumb dogs, they cannot bark; sleeping, lying down, loving to slumber; yea, they are greedy dogs, which can never have enough, and they are shepherds that cannot understand: they all look to their own way, every one for his gain, from his quarter."

Here Samuel ended the quotation, and the three gentlemen left without ceremony.

Source: Lucy Mack Smith, *History of Joseph Smith by His Mother* (Salt Lake City: Stevens & Wallis, Inc., 1945), 162–163

Mother Whitmer and the Angel

One of the most sacred sites of Mormonism is the Peter Whitmer Cabin in Fayette, New York. It was here that the Book of Mormon translation was completed. It was here that three men were chosen as special witnesses and granted the opportunity to converse with an angel, view the plates, and hear the witness of God regarding the Book of Mormon. It was also here that The Church of Jesus Christ of Latter-day Saints was organized on April 6, 1830. And it was here that many other great revelations were received. Considering the incalculable souls eternally blessed by what happened here, truly this is a holy place where the mercy of God was abundant.

But there was a time when this glorious future almost didn't happen here. Joseph Smith came to Fayette in June 1829 at the encouragement of Peter and Mary Whitmer—whose home and farm it was. They generously provided the Prophet an upper room in which to translate. It was the food at their table and the place to sleep they provided that sustained life while the work progressed.

With Joseph came Emma and Oliver Cowdery, as well as an innumerable train of visitors and the curious, which weighted the burden on Mother Whitmer, who felt the responsibility to care for them all. One day she was particularly tired. She went outside to attend to the evening chores and milk the cow. As she did, she saw Joseph and Oliver nearby skipping rocks across the pond—an activity they often did to relax and relieve the tedium of translation. The whole thing annoyed her; she thought to herself that they might just as well chop some wood or carry a bucket of water as skip rocks, and according to her family, she was about to order them from the home.

As she came out of the barn carrying two buckets of milk, she was met by a stranger—an old, heavyset man with a knapsack on his back. At first, she was frightened, but—

> . . . when he spoke to her in a kind, friendly tone
> and began to explain to her the nature of the work
> which was going on in her house, she was filled
> with unexpressible joy and satisfaction. He then
> untied his knapsack and showed her a bundle of
> plates, which in size and appearance corresponded
> with the description subsequently given by the wit-
> nesses to the Book of Mormon. This strange person
> turned the leaves of the book of plates over, leaf
> after leaf, and also showed her the engravings upon
> them; after which he told her to be patient and
> faithful in bearing her burden a little longer, prom-
> ising that if she would do so, she should be blessed;

44

and her reward would be sure, if she proved faithful to the end. The personage then suddenly vanished with the plates, and where he went, she could not tell. From that moment [Mother Whitmer] was enabled to perform her household duties with comparative ease, and she felt no more inclination to murmur because her lot was hard.

Source: Royal Skousen, "Another Account of Mary Whitmer's Viewing of the Golden Plates," *Interpreter: A Journal of Mormon Scripture*, Vol. 10 (2014), 35–44

Mary Musselman, born August 27, 1778, in Germany. She immigrated to Pennsylvania, where she married Peter Whitmer Sr. sometime before 1798. By 1800 she lived in Lebanon Township, Dauphin County, Pennsylvania, and she moved to Fayette, Seneca County, New York, by 1809. A member of the German Reformed Church, Mary was baptized a member of The Church of Jesus Christ of Latter-day Saints by Oliver Cowdery on April 18, 1830, in Fayette. She moved to an area near Kirtland, Geauga County, Ohio, in 1831 and settled in Hiram, Portage County, Ohio. During the next six years, she moved to Jackson County, Missouri (1832); Clay County, Missouri (around late 1833); Far West, Caldwell County, Missouri (by 1838); and to Richmond, Ray County, Missouri (1838). Mary died in January 1856 at Richmond.

Source: Mary Musselman Whitmer, *josephsmithpapers.org*

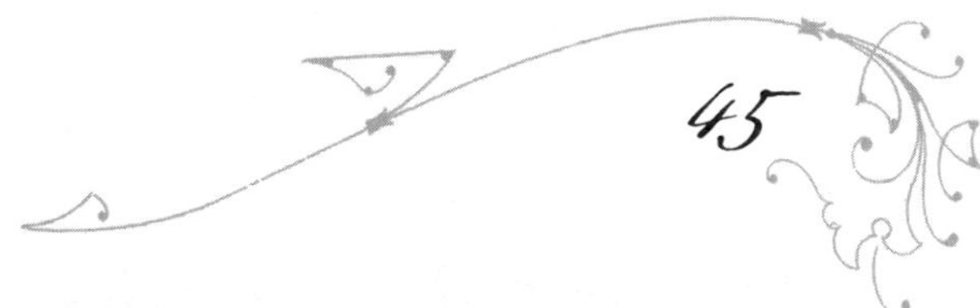

Oliver Cowdery

Oliver Cowdery and the Restoration of the Aaronic Priesthood

On March 31, 1829, Oliver Cowdery set out with Samuel Harrison Smith to journey 129 miles to Harmony, Pennsylvania. Oliver, having seen a vision of the gold plates in possession of Joseph Smith Jr., knew of the truthfulness of the work Joseph was doing and was determined to help.

The journey was difficult. Spring was late in coming, and the season was wet and cold.

Oliver's toes were nipped by frost.

Upon arrival, Oliver and Joseph spent much of the first night talking. After talking to him personally, Oliver was even more convinced that Joseph was telling the truth, and he agreed to be Joseph's scribe.

By April 7, 1829, they began in the book of Mosiah and moved forward. By the middle of May, they had reached 3 Nephi. It was a difficult time for them, as there was little food to sustain them. They had to stop so they could look for work and food.

May 15, 1829, dawned wet and cold. By that date they had written the account of the Savior's visit to the Nephites. The vital importance of proper authority in administering the ordinances of salvation impressed them. It was obvious that not just anyone could act for the Lord, something they had never before supposed. They decided to pray about it.

The two went out into a wooded area on the north part of Joseph's farm—a place called "the Sugar Bush"—where they knelt to pray. In the middle of their prayer, in the brightness of the day, an angel descended in a cloud of light. His voice, though mild, pierced them to the center, and his words dispelled their every fear. He told Joseph and Oliver that he was John the Baptist and that he had been sent by Peter, James, and John. He then laid his hands upon them and conferred upon them the Aaronic Priest-hood, saying:

> Upon you my fellow servants, in the name of
> Messiah I confer the Priesthood of Aaron, which
> holds the keys of the ministering of angels, and
> of the gospel of repentance, and of baptism by
> immersion for the remission of sins; and this shall
> never be taken again from the earth, until the
> sons of Levi do offer again an offering unto the
> Lord in righteousness. (D&C 13:1)

Joseph and Oliver were then told that they would later receive the higher or Melchizedek Priesthood. John then commanded Joseph and Oliver to baptize each other. They went from the woods down to the Susquehanna River that flowed through the property.

The Susquehanna was a busy commercial river; thousands traversed it by barge every spring. Records of the time indicate that the river was flooding that year. It was deep and cold and flowing with ice on the day that Joseph and Oliver were baptized.

Joseph first baptized Oliver, whereupon he came up out of the water and, filled with the Holy Ghost, began to prophesy. Oliver then baptized Joseph, and Joseph was also filled with the Spirit of the Lord and began to prophesy. Then, according to John's instructions, Joseph ordained Oliver to the Aaronic Priesthood, following which Oliver ordained Joseph.

Oliver would later write of this occasion:

> I shall not attempt to paint to you the feelings of this heart, nor the majestic beauty and glory which surrounded us on this occasion; but you will believe me when I say, that earth, nor men, with the eloquence of time, cannot begin to clothe language in as interesting and sublime a manner as this holy personage. Nor has this earth the power to give the joy, to bestow the peace, or comprehend the wisdom which was contained in each sentence as they were delivered by the power of the Holy Spirit.

Oliver would speak in awe of that moment for the rest of his days:

I have been sensitive on this subject, I admit; but I ought to be so—you would be, under the circumstances, had you stood in the presence of John, with our departed brother Joseph, to receive the Lesser Priesthood—and in the presence of Peter, to receive the Greater, and look down through time, and witness the effects these two must produce. (*Letter of Oliver Cowdery to Phineas H. Young, Tiffin, Ohio, March 23, 1846*, Church Archives)

Sources: History of the Saints interview with Mark Lyman Staker, November 26, 2013

Larry C. Porter, "Dating the Restoration of the Melchizedek Priesthood," *Ensign*, June 1979, *churchofjesuschrist.org*

Oliver Cowdery, the son of William Cowdery and Rebecca Fuller, was born October 3, 1806, at Wells, Rutland County, Vermont. He was raised Congregationalist. Oliver moved to western New York and clerked at a store 1825–1828. A clerk, teacher, justice of the peace, lawyer, and newspaper editor, he taught a term as local schoolmaster at Manchester, Ontario County, New York, 1828–1829. In 1829, Oliver assisted Joseph Smith as the principal scribe during translation of the Book of Mormon. With Joseph Smith,

Oliver was baptized and received priesthood authority in 1829. Oliver moved to Fayette, Seneca County, New York, and was one of the Three Witnesses of the Book of Mormon in June 1829. He helped oversee the printing of the Book of Mormon by E. B. Grandin in 1829–1830 and was among six original members of The Church of Jesus Christ of Latter-day Saints, baptized on April 6, 1830.

Oliver was excommunicated in 1838 and moved to Richmond, Ray County, Missouri, that summer. He returned to Kirtland in 1838, where he briefly practiced law. He moved to Tiffin, Seneca County, Ohio, where he continued practicing law and held political offices from 1840–1847. Oliver moved to Elkhorn, Walworth County, Wisconsin Territory, in 1847, where he ran unsuccessfully for the Wisconsin State Assembly in 1848. Oliver requested and received readmission to The Church of Jesus Christ of Latter-day Saints in 1848 at Kanesville (later Council Bluffs), Pottawattamie County, Iowa. Oliver died March 3, 1850, at Richmond, Ray County, Missouri.

Source: Oliver Cowdery, *josephsmithpapers.org*

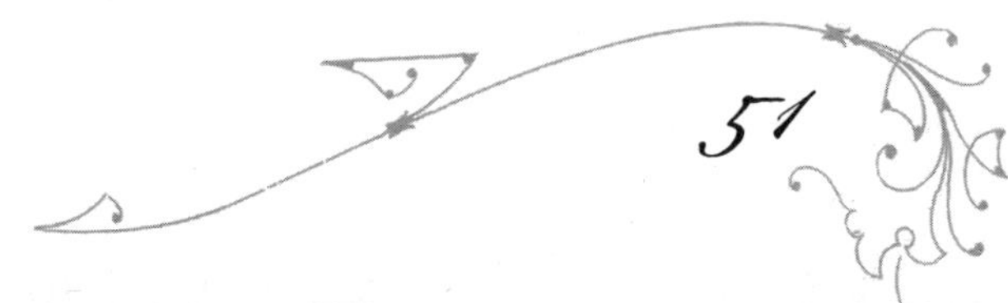

Orrin Porter Rockwell

Porter's Pennies

By 1829 in Manchester, New York, twenty-three-year-old Joseph Smith Jr. had completed the translation of the Book of Mormon. It had taken considerable doing, but he had finally persuaded Egbert Bratt Grandin of Palmyra, a young entrepreneur, to print the book. Grandin had agreed to print five thousand copies at the exorbitant price of $3,000. Even so, he was extremely reluctant to take the project, believing the book would not sell and he would not be paid. Because of that, the terms of the contract were stiff in Grandin's favor.

Joseph and his family did not have that kind of money. Fortunately, Martin Harris was able to mortgage his farm to secure the printing of the book. Even so, money and means to pay for the printing of the Book of Mormon were scarce and precious.

Orrin Porter Rockwell was just a lad of about sixteen at the time. His family and the Smith family were close, and he remembered Father and Mother Smith coming over to visit—

visits during which they shared the marvelous developments
of the Restoration. Porter believed their every word. He looked
forward to those visits and begged his parents to let him stay up
and be part of the discussions. He even tended the pine torch that
illuminated those nightly discussions.

When Porter learned that Joseph needed money to print the
Book of Mormon, he determined to help in any way he could.
While his prospects were limited, he was very creative. After his
day's work, he went into the woods and picked berries by moon-
light, which he sold in the village. He gave the money to Joseph.
When the berries ran out, he gathered wood and hauled that to
town to sell.

No man ever loved the Prophet Joseph Smith more than Porter. "His heart was devoted to the cause of truth . . . and he would
not have hesitated to give his life for Joseph at any time"—a fact
he proved again and again until Joseph was taken for the last time.

Porter was true to the end of his days. When he died in June
1878, he was the most senior Church member still alive. The
epitaph of Orrin Porter Rockwell reads, "He was brave and loyal to
his faith, true to the prophet Jos. Smith."

Source: Mark L. McConkie, *Remembering Joseph: Personal Recollections of
Those Who Knew the Prophet Joseph Smith* (Salt Lake City: Deseret Book,
2003), 299

Orrin Porter Rockwell, the son of Orin Rockwell and Sarah Witt, was born in June 1814 in Belchertown, Hampshire County, Massachusetts. A ferry operator, herdsman, and farmer, he was a neighbor to Joseph Smith and was baptized a member of The Church of Jesus Christ of Latter-day Saints in 1830 in Ontario County. Porter married Luana Beebe on February 2, 1832, in Jackson County. He was imprisoned in Missouri in March of 1843 on suspicion of attempting to kill former Missouri Governor Lilburn W. Boggs. Orrin was admitted to the Council of Fifty on March 19, 1844, and was ordained a high priest before January 5, 1846. He migrated with Brigham Young's vanguard pioneer company to the Salt Lake Valley in 1847. Porter married Mary Ann Neff; she died September 28, 1866. He later married Christine Olsen. Porter died June 9, 1878, in Salt Lake City.

Source: Orrin Porter Rockwell, *josephsmithpapers.org*

55

Joseph Smith Sr. by Annie Henrie Nader © By Intellectual Reserve, Inc.

Joseph Smith Sr.

"Remember Faith": Joseph Smith Sr.

In February 1829, notwithstanding the snow and cold, Joseph Smith Sr.—now in his fifty-eighth year—arrived in Harmony, Pennsylvania, with his son Samuel to visit his other son, Joseph Smith Jr. and his wife Emma. The work of translating the Book of Mormon was underway but was progressing slowly.

In the course of that visit, Father Smith humbly "desired to know what the Lord had for him to do." Joseph the Seer inquired of the Lord, and this significant revelation followed:

> Now behold, a marvelous work is about to come forth among the children of men.
>
> Therefore, O ye that embark in the service of God, see that ye serve him with all your heart, might, mind, and strength, that ye may stand blameless before God at the last day.
>
> Therefore, if ye have desires to serve God ye are called to the work. (D&C 4:1–3)

The revelation continued; we know it as Doctrine and Covenants 4.

We have no record of Father Smith's immediate reaction to that revelation. However, some months later, after the Book of Mormon was published, a Quaker man came to Father Smith's home and announced that he had purchased a note—a debt— against Father Smith, and he was there to collect. When Father Smith asked the man why he had bought a debt that was not his own, the Quaker refused to answer. Father Smith offered him six dollars, promising that the rest would follow if the man would wait. The man's response is telling:

"No," he said, "I will not wait one hour; and if [you do] not pay me immediately, [you] shall go forthwith to the jail, unless, (and he ran to the fire place and made violent gestures with his hands towards the fire), [you] will burn up them Books of Mormon. But, if [you] will burn them up, then I will forgive [you] the whole debt."

To this Father Smith answered decidedly, "That I shall not do."

"Then," answered the Quaker, "[you] shall go to the jail."

At this point, Lucy Mack Smith offered her gold beads that were worth enough to pay the remainder of the debt, but the man refused them. Instead, he called in a waiting constable, who arrested Father Smith and took him to jail.

Along the way, Father Smith's captors made him this offer: "The men by whom I was taken," he said, "commenced using every possible argument to induce me to renounce the Book of Mor- mon; saying how much better it would be for you to deny that silly thing, than to be disgraced, and imprisoned, when you might, not only escape, but also have the note back; as well as the money you have paid on it."

Father Smith refused the offer, was locked in a cell with a murderer, and was kept in prison for the next thirty days. While a prisoner, he kept the faith and preached the restored gospel. Upon his release, he baptized two into the Church.

In the revelation first given to Father Smith in 1829, two qualities are mentioned twice as qualifying one for the work of God: faith and charity. Notwithstanding his weaknesses, they seem to characterize the remainder of the days of Joseph Smith Sr.

Sources: *Joseph Smith Papers, Documents,* Volume 1

Lucy Mack Smith, History, 1845, page 185, *josephsmithpapers.org*

Joseph Smith Sr., the son of Asael Smith and Mary Duty, was born July 2, 1771, at Topsfield, Essex County, Massachusetts. A cooper, farmer, teacher, and merchant, he was a nominal member of the Congregationalist Church at Topsfield. Joseph was married to Lucy Mack in a ceremony performed by Seth Austin on January 24, 1796, at Tunbridge, Orange County, Vermont. In June 1839, Joseph was one of the Eight Witnesses of the Book of Mormon, and he was baptized a member of The Church of Jesus Christ of Latter-day Saints by Oliver Cowdery on April 6, 1830. He

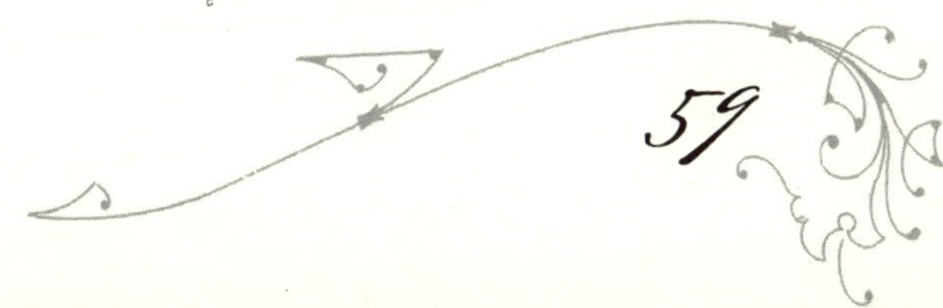

was ordained patriarch of the Church and assistant president on December 6, 1834. When the Saints were expelled from Missouri, Joseph migrated to Quincy, Adams County, Illinois, in February 1839. In the spring of 1839, he moved to Commerce (later Nauvoo), Hancock County, Illinois. Joseph died September 14, 1840, at Nauvoo.

Source: Joseph Smith Sr., *josephsmithpapers.org*

Angels in the Room

When Sallie Heller Conrad took the job in 1829, she hadn't planned on this.

Sallie was about eighteen years old and hired to help a busy mother around the house. The home was small, and in addition to the large family already living there, guests were also living at the house.

In the course of her duties, Sallie quickly figured out that something was going on upstairs. One day Sallie noticed a couple of young men come down from the second story. They looked most unusual. Their faces were "exceedingly white and strange." She asked the family why they looked that way, but no one would tell her. It seemed to be some kind of secret.

As time passed the same thing happened again and again, and each time Sallie saw them, their faces were that same unearthly white. It frightened her. Finally, she went to the lady of the house and announced "that she would not stay with her until she knew the cause of the strange looks of these men."

The lady of the house was Mother Mary Whitmer of Fayette, New York. Mother Whitmer explained to Sallie that those two

men—Joseph Smith and Oliver Cowdery—were translating an ancient record written on gold plates by the gift and power of God, and "that the power of God was so great in the room that they could hardly endure it; at times angels were in the room in their glory, which nearly consumed them."

This explanation satisfied Sallie and opened the way to her embracing the gospel. Sallie Heller Conrad married in the faith, came west, and died in Provo, Utah, July 23, 1903. She was ninety-two years old.

Source: Mark L. McConkie, *Remembering Joseph: Personal Recollections of Those Who Knew the Prophet Joseph Smith* (Salt Lake City: Deseret Book, 2003), 248

Sarah Helen "Sallie" Conrad was born September 19, 1810, in Elmira, Chemung County, New York. She attended the meeting at the Whitmer cabin where the Church was organized on April 6, 1830. Sarah married David Bunnell in April 1830 and was baptized a member of The Church of Jesus Christ of Latter-day Saints on September 21, 1831. She emigrated to Utah with their eight children. Sarah died July 23, 1903, in Provo, Utah County, Utah, and is buried in the Provo City Cemetery.

Source: Sarah Helen "Sallie" Conrad Bunnell, Memorial, *www.findagrave.com*

The Early Years of Oliver Cowdery

Oliver Cowdery was born in Wells, Rutland County, Vermont, October 3, 1806, the youngest child of William and Rebecca Fuller Cowdery. When he was only three, his mother passed away. He was sent to live with an aunt and uncle, but they too passed away.

His father remarried Keziah Pierce Austin and three more children were born to the family; one of those children, Lucy, later married Phineas Young, the brother of Brigham Young. As he grew, Oliver received an exceptionally good education.

Around 1827, Oliver made his way to Lyons, New York, not too far from Palmyra. In October 1828, Oliver's brother, Lyman Cowdery, was appointed the school teacher in the Palmyra area, but another commitment forced him to withdraw. He encouraged the school board to appoint his younger brother Oliver to the position. Oliver received the appointment.

Among those on the board that appointed Oliver was Hyrum Smith. Because Oliver was single, he asked to board with the Smith family. Records show that there were 107 students enrolled in the school, among them the Smith children.

By November 1828, Oliver heard the rumors of Joseph Smith
and the "Gold Bible," and he was intrigued. At the same time, he
formed a friendship with David Whitmer, and the two of them
wanted to know more. Oliver inquired of the Smith family, but
they were reluctant to discuss it with anyone. Finally, Father Smith
shared the story with Oliver.

Oliver would later say, "it was working in my bones and I
couldn't think of anything else." Oliver determined that as soon as
the term of his contract for teaching school was up, he would go
to Pennsylvania and scribe for Joseph as he translated the Book of
Mormon. Lucy Mack Smith recorded that "from this time Oliver
was so entirely absorbed in the subject of the record that it seemed
impossible for him to think, or converse about anything else."

Oliver's convictions and determination to help Joseph came
from more than a passing whim. Joseph later said, "The Lord
appeared unto a young man by the name of Oliver Cowdery and
shewed unto him the plates in a vision, and also the truth of the
work and what the Lord was about to do through me his unworthy
servant. Therefore he was desirous to come and write for me."

As spring 1829 approached, the Smiths were forced to move
out of their frame home they had built and back into the small log
cabin in which they had once lived. Thinking the accommodations
would be too tight for Oliver, Lucy suggested that he might look
for lodging elsewhere. "Mother," Oliver exclaimed with much feeling, "only let me stay with you and I can live in any log hut where
you and Father live, but I cannot go away from you. So say no
more about convenience; I care not for it. I can do well enough."

Finally, on March 31, 1829, after months of anticipation and with the school term ended, Oliver set out for Harmony, Pennsylvania, with his $65 stipend in his pocket. Joseph's brother Samuel accompanied him. They arrived in Harmony on April 5, 1829. Two days later, Oliver began to scribe for Joseph, assisting him in the work of translating the Book of Mormon.

Source: History of the Saints Interview with Alexander L. Baugh, January 2014

Oliver Cowdery by Annie Henrie Nader © By Intellectual Reserve, Inc.

Oliver Cowdery

David Whitmer

Martin Harris

Three Sure Witnesses

It was a pleasant summer day in late June 1829 in the small community of Fayette, New York. About eleven in the morning, Joseph Smith, Martin Harris, and Oliver Cowdery walked from the home of Peter Whitmer III into a nearby field where their companion David Whitmer was plowing. Together they went into the woods about forty rods from the cabin.

At that distance, they sat down on a log, talked for a while, and then knelt and began to pray in faith—each in turn—that they could see the plates from which the Book of Mormon had been translated. Joseph prayed first. At the conclusion of the first round, they then prayed again, but still there was no result. At that point, Martin Harris proposed that he withdraw himself.

After Martin left, they knelt and prayed again. They had not been many minutes in prayer when they discovered "a light above [them] in the air of exceeding brightness." With the light "came a strange entrancing influence which permeated [them] so powerfully

that [they] felt chained to the spot." It was accompanied with a "sensation of joy absolutely indescribable."

Standing before them was an angel of the Lord, holding in his hands the gold plates from which the Book of Mormon had been translated. He turned the leaves of the record one by one so that they were visible to every man present. Addressing David Whitmer, he said, "David, blessed is the Lord, and he that keepeth his commandments."

Immediately afterward, they heard a voice from out of the bright light above them saying, "These plates have been revealed by the power of God, and they have been translated by the power of God. They translation of them which you have seen is correct, and I command you to bear record of what you now see and hear."

There appeared about three feet away "a table, with many records on it—besides the plates of the Book of Mormon, also the sword of Laban, the Directors, and the interpreters." David would later declare that "human language could not describe [the] heavenly things and that which we saw."

At the close of the vision, Joseph went in search of Martin Harris. Upon finding him, Martin asked Joseph to join him in prayer. Before they had finished their prayer, the same vision was opened again. Upon hearing and beholding the vision, "Martin Harris cried out, apparently in ecstasy of joy, 'Tis enough; mine eyes have beheld,' and jumping up he shouted hosanna, blessing God, and otherwise rejoiced exceedingly."

The four men returned to the cabin and drafted a document that stands today in the front of the Book of Mormon. It begins, "Be it known unto all nations, kindreds, tongues, and people unto whom this work shall come. . . ." It is the testimony of the Three Witnesses. Theirs is a profound example of an irrevocable law of God from the beginning: "that in the mouth of two or three witnesses every word may be established" (Matthew 18:16).

Source: A Composite Interview with David Whitmer, *scottwoodward.org*

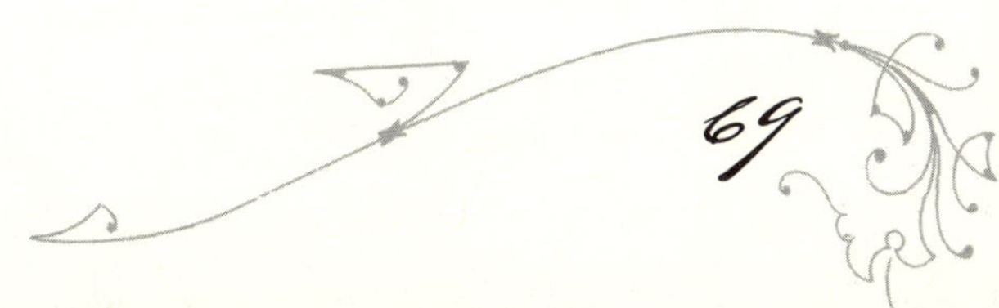

Thurlow Weed

He Refused to Print the Book of Mormon

Born to farmers in 1797 in Greene County, New York, Thurlow Weed served in the War of 1812 while just a lad, rising to the rank of quartermaster sergeant. Later he worked his way up the ranks in the newspaper business. Through that work he became interested in politics and was elected at the young age of twenty-seven to the New York State Assembly, where he served for many years.

Through the skillful use of the press and a shrewd understanding of the political machine, he became an indomitable force in New York politics—at one time becoming the absolute boss of the Whig Party in New York. He was considered a master organizer, maintaining strict control of the Whig Party in New York even as it came apart throughout the rest of the Union. At one time his newspaper had the largest circulation of any political newspaper in America. Though he had strong political ideals, he was personable and popular. Among other things, he opposed slavery.

In 1840, Weed backed William Henry Harrison for President of the United States. Harrison won, but died shortly after taking office. He backed General Zachary Taylor for President in 1848, but Taylor too died in office. Then came the presidential campaign of 1860, in which Weed backed an old friend from New York whose election seemed a sure thing—William H. Seward. But the nomination and the presidency went to Abraham Lincoln. Weed threw all his support behind Lincoln and was a trusted envoy until he disagreed with the President over the Emancipation Proclamation of 1862. He eventually fell from favor with his party and retired from politics. He died in New York City in relative obscurity, blind and suffering from chronic vertigo, in 1882.

How many people today remember Thurlow Weed and honor his memory? His name is likely as obscure today as it was when he died—which makes it likely that not many have heard "the rest of the story," one that involves a decision that could have given him great notoriety.

In July and August of 1829 Joseph Smith, Oliver Cowdery, and Martin Harris were looking for someone willing and able to undertake a huge printing project—five thousand copies of a 588-page book bound in leather: the Book of Mormon. Before they ever signed a contract with twenty-three-year-old Egbert B. Grandin, they approached another printer—one in the area of Rochester, New York, who was much more skilled and experienced than Grandin.

Joseph approached the experienced printer twice, asking for his help. But the master printer ridiculed both the man and the book. "I thought [Joseph Smith] . . . a very shallow imposter," he later said, "and therefore declined to become a publisher, thus depriving myself of whatever notoriety might have been achieved by having my name imprinted upon the title page of the first Mormon bible."

That printer who mocked the latter-day Prophet and the revealed word of God, the one who rejected the eternal honor of first printing the Book of Mormon, was none other than Thurlow Weed.

Sources: History of the Saints Interview with Gerrit Dirkmaat, June 2013
Thurlow Weed, *en.wikipedia.org*

Thurlow Weed, born in Cairo, New York, on November 15, 1797, was a New York newspaper publisher and politician in the Whig and Republican parties. He was the principal political advisor to prominent New York politician William H. Seward and was instrumental in the Presidential nominations of William Henry Harrison (1840), Zachary Taylor (1848), and John C. Frémont (1856).

Thurlow served in the War of 1812 and apprenticed for newspapers before winning election to the New York State Assembly. He helped organize the Republican Party and supported Frémont's nomination at the 1856 Republican National Convention. He led the effort to nominate Seward at the 1860 Republican National Convention, but the convention nominated Abraham Lincoln instead. After the Civil War, Weed and Seward allied with President Andrew Johnson and supported Johnson's approach to Reconstruction. Weed retired from public life in 1867 and died November 22, 1882.

Source: Thurlow Weed, *en.wikipedia.org*

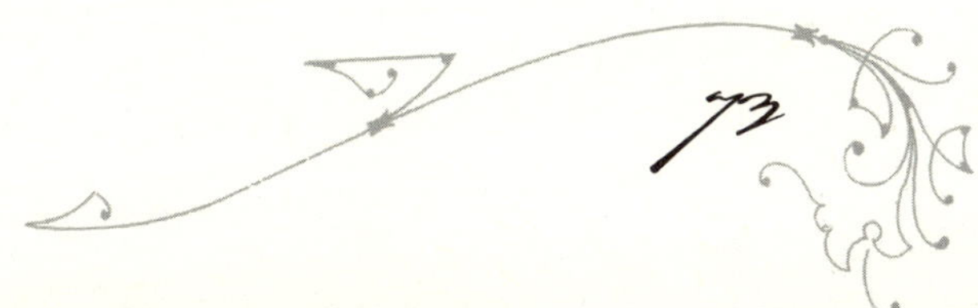

Translating the Book of Mormon,
by Kirt Harmon

Voices from the Dust

Paul the Apostle wrote that "God hath chosen the foolish things of the world to confound the wise; and God hath chosen the weak things of the world to confound the things which are mighty" (1 Corinthians 1:27). Perhaps that was never more true than in the case of Joseph Smith and the Book of Mormon.

Joseph Smith's wife, Emma, wrote that Joseph Smith

> could neither write nor dictate a coherent and well-worded letter; let alone dictating a book like the Book of Mormon. And though I was an active participant in the scenes that transpired, and was present during the translation of the plates, and had cognizance of things as they transpired, it is marvelous to me, 'a marvel and a wonder' as much so as to anyone else.

Along with others, Emma watched the Book of Mormon come forth from Joseph's dictation. Those who watched the translation

knew him; they also knew without doubt that the Book of Mormon came from God. It could not have come from Joseph.

David Whitmer witnessed the translation for himself and wrote:

> Joseph Smith would put the seer stone into a hat and put his face in the hat, drawing it close around his face to exclude the light. And in the darkness the spiritual light would shine. A piece of something resembling parchment would appear, and on that appeared the writing. One character at a time would appear, and under it was the interpretation in English. Brother Joseph would read off the English to Oliver Cowdery who was his principal scribe. And when it was written down and repeated to Brother Joseph to see if it was correct, then it would disappear and another character with the interpretation would appear. Thus the Book of Mormon was translated by the gift and power of God and not by any power of man.

Joseph Knight Sr. was also a witness to the translation process and recorded this in his history:

> [Joseph] put the Urim and Thummim into his hat and darkened his eyes. A sentence would appear in bright Roman letters, then he would tell the writer and he would write it. And then that would go away. And the next sentence would come, and so on. But if it was not spelled right, it

would not go away until it was right. And so we see it was marvelous.

To us, the Book of Mormon is a marvelous work and a wonder because of what it says and the influence it has on us, but to that founding generation there was another dimension. They marveled and wondered at how the book came forth. How could an ignorant and unlearned farmer dictate before their very eyes such marvelous words as they heard Joseph speak? They knew the book was true simply by the miracle of its production. Emma Smith wrote:

> I am satisfied that no man could have dictated the writing of the manuscript unless he was inspired; for when acting as his scribe, [Joseph] would dictate to me hour after hour; and when returning after meals, or after interruptions, he would at once begin where he had left off, without either seeing the manuscript or having any portion of it read to him. This was a usual thing for him to do. It would have been improbable that a learned man could do this; and for one so ignorant and unlearned as he was, it was simply impossible.

The Book of Mormon *is* a miracle. Voices from the dust—not only Nephi, Jacob, Mormon, and others, but also Joseph, Emma, David, Martin, Oliver, and many others involved in the Restoration—declare the truth, telling us that the Book of Mormon came from God.

Source: History of the Saints, *The Miracle of the Book of Mormon* (DVD)

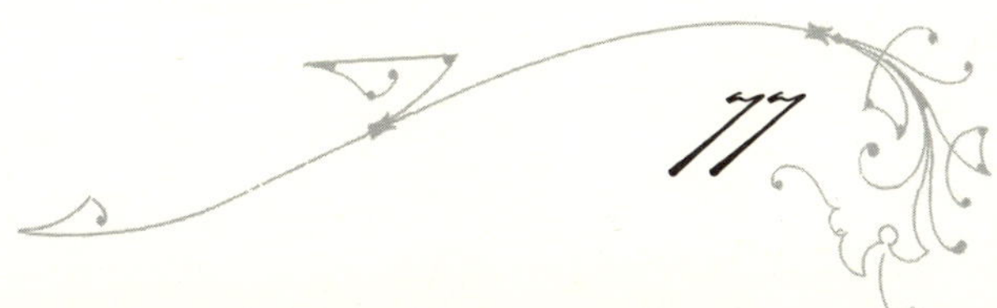

77

David Whitmer, the son of Peter Whitmer Sr. and Mary Musselman, was born January 7, 1805, near Harrisburg, Dauphin County, Pennsylvania. A farmer and livery keeper, he was baptized by Joseph Smith in June 1829 in Seneca Lake, Seneca County, New York. One of the Three Witnesses of the Book of Mormon in 1829, he was among six original members of the Church and was ordained an elder on April 6, 1830. David married Julia Ann Jolly on January 9, 1831, at Seneca County. He was rejected as Church president in meetings at Far West, Missouri, February 5–9, 1838, and was excommunicated April 13, 1838, at Far West. Expelled from Far West in late June 1838, he moved to Clay County and then to Richmond, Ray County, Missouri, where he operated a livery stable. Elected mayor of Richmond 1867–1868, he founded the Church of Christ (Whitmerite) in 1875. David later set forth his religious claims in *An Address to All Believers in Christ, by a Witness to the Divine Authenticity of the Book of Mormon,* published in 1887. David died January 25, 1888, in Richmond.

Lucy and
the Strangers

O n October 10, 1830, in a small town in Ohio, fifteen-year-old Lucy sat in the home of her employer, Mrs. Abigail Daniels, tending to her weaving when a knock sounded at the door. When young Lucy opened the door, there stood "three well-dressed, nice looking gentlemen." Lucy invited them in, got them some chairs, and took their hats.

As soon as the young men were seated, they began to share a remarkable message that the gospel of Jesus Christ had been revealed anew. Angels had appeared and given authority for the gospel to be preached once more upon the earth, they said.

Suddenly the lady of the house turned from her work at the loom, shuttle in hand, and shook it in their faces. She told them to leave her house immediately, as she would not have her children polluted with such doctrine. She called them impostors and deceivers and ordered them to leave. They tried to reason with her, but to no avail.

They then explained that they were very hungry and had eaten nothing all day. Notwithstanding the unspoken rules of frontier hospitality, she said, "I have plenty, but nothing for you."

At that point, Lucy could take no more. "I had been sitting there all this time listening to her foul tongue. I could stand it no longer, for I felt that they were the servants of God as they said they were," she wrote.

"Gentlemen," she told the young men, "my father lives one mile from here. He never turns anyone hungry from his door. Go there and you will be fed and cared for." With that, Lucy gave them their hats and led them outside. She showed them the road and gave directions to her father's house and watched until they were out of sight.

When Lucy went back in the house, Mrs. Daniels turned her anger on the girl, but no matter. Those missionaries went to Lucy's father; as she had promised, he welcomed them, fed them, and listened to them. As a result, his household, including Lucy, along with many others were converted and baptized, becoming some of the earliest converts to the restored gospel of Jesus Christ in Kirtland, Ohio.

The three young strangers who shared the gospel message that day were Oliver Cowdery, Parley P. Pratt, and Ziba Peterson. Lucy, the young girl who came to their aid, was Lucy Diantha Morley. Her father was Isaac Morley, the founder of the settlement of the San Pete in Utah and the great patriarch in the faith of a numerous posterity.

Source: Autobiography of Lucy Diantha Morley Allen, Church History Library

Lucy Morley was born October 4, 1815, in Kirtland, Lake County, Ohio, to Isaac Morley and Lucy Gunn Morley. She married Joseph Stewart Allen September 2, 1835, in Clay County, Missouri. She was a close friend of the Prophet Joseph Smith, who stayed with her father, Isaac Morley. She was driven with the Saints from place to place until she arrived in Utah in 1848. Lucy helped settle Manti with her husband and her father. At five feet five inches with black hair and eyes, she was gentle, meek, loving, and kind and was the mother of twelve.

Source: Lucy Diantha Morley Allen, Memorial, *findagrave.com*

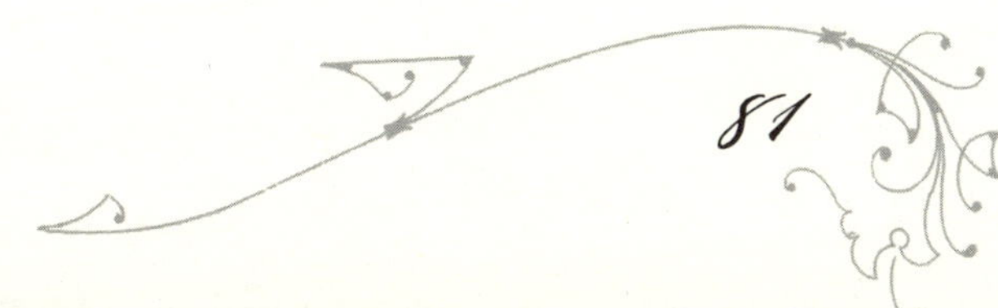

Martin Harris by Annie Henrie Nader © By Intellectual Reserve, Inc.

He Put It All on the Line

artin Harris was a man raised up for a singular purpose, called and chosen to assist in the bringing forth of the Book of Mormon. His was a family of English Quakers who emigrated to Palmyra, New York, at the end of the eighteenth century. They settled on six hundred acres just north of the Palmyra townsite and turned it into some of the best farmland in the area.

Martin married his first cousin Lucy Harris and they raised a family. By 1825, their marriage was so strained that they legally divided their property and moved into separate households, though they continued amicable association as far as possible.

Joseph Smith received a revelation through the Urim and Thummim that Martin was to be the man to assist in bringing forth the Book of Mormon. And so it was that in the summer of 1829, when the Book of Mormon was ready to be printed— five thousand copies at the astonishing price of $3,000—Martin stepped forward and offered his farm as collateral for the printing.

At that time $3,000 was a fortune, and no one other than Martin had the faith and means to support such an undertaking. Imagine what must have gone through his mind on August 25, 1829, when Martin signed the agreement with Egbert B. Grandin. The agreement stipulated that if book sales did not sufficiently compensate Grandin, Martin would sell his farm to pay the debt.

This was no ordinary farm. Martin had built one of the most coveted farms in all of Palmyra. He was a prosperous and well-respected member of the community. And now all of that was on the line—his farm was mortgaged to Grandin, and his reputation hung on Joseph Smith and the Book of Mormon. But Martin believed in what he was doing; he was confident that when the book came off the press, sales would surely square the debt and he could keep his farm.

In March 1830, the first copies of the Book of Mormon were finished. His arms loaded with books, Martin went throughout the community soliciting sales, but the angry, hard-hearted citizens of Palmyra held true to a threatened boycott, and the books did not sell. It was quickly becoming evident to Martin that this endeavor would cost him his life's work. In February 1831, the agreement with Grandin came due, and Martin sold his farm to a family friend, Thomas Lakey, for $3,000.

History has not been particularly kind to Martin Harris, but say whatever you like—he willingly paid for the Book of Mormon, and by that sacrifice obtained a faith in the book that lasted the rest of his life. Joseph the Seer translated it. Oliver Cowdery wrote every word that came from Joseph's mouth. But what good would their work do if no one could read it?

Think for a moment of the good those first five thousand books accomplished. They brought an entire generation to the Savior and His restored gospel. Just one of those books today is worth more than all Martin originally gave for the lot.

Though Martin could not have known it at the time, he gave his land for a legacy, and he sacrificed his reputation among men for a greater reputation in heaven. As long as the Book of Mormon continues to bring men to worship the risen Christ, the name of Martin Harris, special witness, will be held in eternal respect, honor, and gratitude.

Source: Agreement with Martin Harris, 16 January 1830, Historical Introduction, *josephsmithpapers.org*

Martin Harris, the son of Nathan Harris and Rhoda Lapham, was born May 18, 1783, at Easton, Albany County, New York. A farmer, in 1793 he moved with his parents to the area of Swift's Landing (later in Palmyra), Ontario County, New York. Martin married his first cousin Lucy Harris on March 27, 1808, in Palmyra. He served in the War of 1812 as a member of the New York militia and became a landowner of some 320 acres at Palmyra. Martin took a transcript of Book of Mormon characters to Luther Bradish, Samuel Latham Mitchill, and Charles Anthon in February 1828 and assisted Joseph Smith as scribe during the translation of the first portion of the Book of Mormon around April 12 to June 14, 1828. Martin was one of the Three Witnesses of the Book

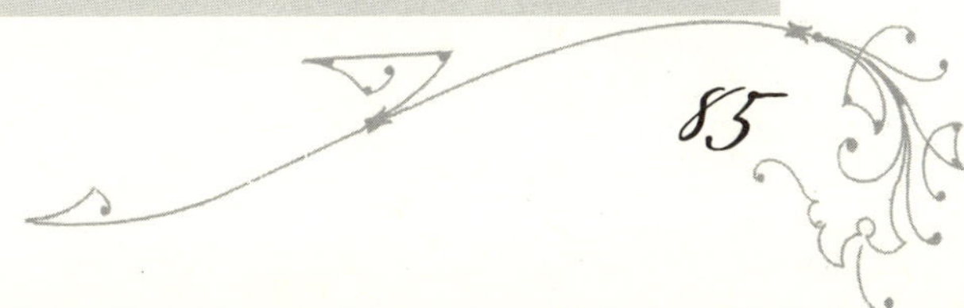

of Mormon in June 1829. Martin was baptized a member of The Church of Jesus Christ of Latter-day Saints by Oliver Cowdery on April 6, 1830; he was ordained a priest by June 9, 1830, and separated from his wife after June 1830. Martin paid the printing costs for publication of the Book of Mormon through sale of 151 acres. He was excommunicated in December 1837 and was rebaptized into The Church of Jesus Christ of Latter-day Saints in 1842 at Kirtland. Martin migrated to the Salt Lake Valley in 1870, where he was rebaptized into the Church that same year. He died July 10, 1875, at Clarkston, Cache County, Utah Territory.

Source: Martin Harris, *josephsmithpapers.org*

Could He Ever Live Up to It?

When Orson was about eighteen years old, his soul was awakened to God. He began to pray very fervently, repenting of every sin. "In the silent shades of night, while others were slumbering upon their pillows, I often retired to some secret place in the lonely fields or solitary wilderness, and bowed before the Lord and prayed for hours with a broken heart and contrite spirit; this was my comfort and delight. The greatest desire of my heart was for the Lord to manifest His will concerning me."

In time, two missionaries came into the area where Orson lived, and one of them was his older brother. As they preached, Orson recognized the truth. On September 19, 1830—his nineteenth birthday—he was baptized, the only individual to do so in that country for many years afterward.

Orson immediately set out on a journey of 230 miles to the west looking for the Prophet Joseph Smith, and by November 4, 1830, he found Joseph at the Father Whitmer cabin in Fayette, New York. After so many years of searching for the Lord and wanting to know His will concerning him, Orson had finally found someone who could tell him.

Orson asked Joseph, and Joseph assured Orson that it was his privilege to know the Lord's will. Joseph invited Orson into the chamber of old Father Whitmer, and with the aid of the seer stone, began to dictate the word and will of Almighty God for Orson Pratt.

When Joseph invited the humble lad to write it down, Orson declined, considering himself not worthy of such a task. Could John Whitmer do it? Yes! And John recorded the revelation we know today as Doctrine and Covenants 34.

In that revelation, Orson was given a promise that to one of such humble origins seemed almost too great to attain. It was, "Lift up your voice and prophesy, and it shall be given by the power of the Holy Ghost." How could he ever live up to that?

Shortly after, he was ordained an elder and sent forth. Notwithstanding his weakness, Orson became one of the most influential leaders of the Church in the nineteenth century. He was always a missionary. He was the first one to enter the Salt Lake Valley in 1847. It was he who from 1876–1879 prepared new editions of the scriptures, adding revelations to the Doctrine and Covenants (such as sections 121–123) and dividing the Book of Mormon into chapters and verses. And there was so much more. On October 3, 1881, after fifty-one years of giving his life to the cause of Christ, Orson Pratt passed away.

What would it have been like to sit at the feet of the Prophet Joseph and have him inquire of the Lord just for us? What is it like to feel as though we are nothing and have little to give—and to have the Lord extend mighty promises, pick us up, square our shoulders, and send us out to work miracles? That we can—and should—all know.

Sources: Revelation, 4 November 1830 [D&C 34], Historical Introduction, *josephsmithpapers.org*

Orson Pratt, *en.wikipedia.org*

Orson Pratt, the son of Jared Pratt and Charity Dickinson, was born September 19, 1811, at Hartford, Washington County, New York. A farmer, writer, teacher, merchant, surveyor, editor, and publisher. Orson was baptized a member of The Church of Jesus Christ of Latter-day Saints by Parley P. Pratt on September 19, 1830, at Canaan. He was ordained an elder by Joseph Smith on December 1, 1830, in Fayette, Seneca County, New York, and was appointed to serve a mission to Colesville, Broome County, New York. Orson was ordained member of the Quorum of the Twelve by David Whitmer and Oliver

Photo courtesy The Church of Jesus Christ of Latter-day Saints

Cowdery on April 26, 1835, at Kirtland. He married Sarah Marinda Bates on July 4, 1836, at Henderson, Jefferson County, New York. Orson served a mission to Upper Canada in 1836 and a mission to Great Britain with other members of Quorum of the Twelve from 1839–1841. Orson entered the Salt Lake Valley with Brigham Young's vanguard pioneer company in 1847. He presided over the Church in Great Britain from 1848–1849 and again from 1856–1857. A member of the Utah territorial legislature, he was appointed Church historian in 1874. Orson died October 3, 1881, at Salt Lake City.

Source: Orson Pratt, *josephsmithpapers.org*

A Date that Signaled the Beginning

Someday in the future when we are beyond this life and can look back on mortality from the vantage point of eternity, as God now does, there will be certain events and dates of greater significance than the world ever knew. They will be those moments that were largely unnoticed, but that will have done the most good for the most people for the greatest amount of time.

Among those dates will surely be March 26, 1830. It was a date that signaled the beginning of a marvelous work that would sweep the entire earth and affect every nation, kindred, tongue, and people.

God Himself marked that moment as a sign to all the world that a great work would commence among all people in which He would gather out from all the nations of the earth the scattered and lost members of the tribes of Israel and restore them to their respective lands of inheritance. That moment was also a stern warning to all the world: "And when ye shall see these sayings coming forth among you, then ye need not any longer spurn at the doings of the Lord, for the sword of his justice is in his right hand,

and behold, at that day, if ye shall spurn at his doings he will cause that it shall soon overtake you" (3 Nephi 29:4).

What was this event that God marked as a sign of a great change? What happened on March 26, 1830? On that date in a small, two-story brick building in Palmyra, New York, the Book of Mormon—a marvelous work and a wonder, a witness and a warning—first went on sale.

Sources: 2 Nephi 30:3–8; 3 Nephi 21, 30

**Grandin Press, Palmyra, courtesy
The Church of Jesus Christ of Latter-day Saints**

Samuel Harrison Smith: By Small and Simple Things

On an evening in June 1830, a circuit preacher named Phineas was on his way home in Mendon, New York. He stopped at the Tomlinson Inn in Mendon for dinner. While he was eating and talking with the family, a roughly dressed stranger, a young man, came up to him holding out a book. "There is a book, Sir, I wish you to read."

Phineas hesitated a moment and then said, "Pray, Sir, what book have you?"

"The Book of Mormon," said the young man, "or, as it is called by some, the Golden Bible."

"Ah, then it purports to be a revelation," Phineas replied.

"Yes," said he. "It is a revelation from God."

Phineas then took the book, which was new. At the young man's direction, Phineas turned to the back of the book and read the testimony of the witnesses. When he finished reading and looked up, the young man said, "If you will read this book with a prayerful heart and ask God to give you a witness, you will know of the truth of this work."

"What is your name?" Phineas asked.

"My name is Samuel Harrison Smith."

"Ah," said Phineas, "you are one of the witnesses."

"Yes. I know the book to be a revelation from God, translated by the gift and power of the Holy Ghost, and that my brother, Joseph Smith, Junior, is a prophet, seer, and revelator."

Skeptical at first, Phineas agreed to read the book, considering it his duty to prove all things and hold fast to that which is good. He read it twice over the next two weeks. Not only did he find it to be without error, but he was converted. He then lent it to his father, who read it and declared it to be "the greatest work . . . he had ever seen." Phineas then gave it to his sister, who read it and declared it to be "a revelation." And so it went down through the family, each in turn believing it to be a new revelation from God.

From that one book came into the Church Phineas, his father, his sister, and all his brothers, including Brigham Young—the second President of the Church—as well as the family of Heber C. Kimball. That small group of believers soon numbered sixty people and formed the Mendon Branch.

Samuel was called and set apart as a missionary just days after the Church was organized. With no training and armed with only a sure testimony and a knapsack full of books, he began his missionary duties. Though he endured much and baptized no one, he changed the world forever, testifying that by small and simple things great things are still brought to pass.

Source: Samuel Smith: Missionary to Prophets, Museum Treasures, *history. churchofjesuschrist.org*

Samuel Harrison Smith, the son of Joseph Smith Sr. and Lucy Mack, was born March 13, 1808, at Tunbridge, Orange County, Vermont. A farmer, logger, scribe, builder, and tavern operator, he was baptized a member of The Church of Jesus Christ of Latter-day Saints by Oliver Cowdery in May 1829 at Harmony (later Oakland), Susquehanna County, Pennsylvania. Samuel was one of the Eight Witnesses of the Book of Mormon in June 1829 and was among the six original members of The Church of Jesus Christ of Latter-day Saints on April 6, 1830. Samuel married Mary Bailey on August 13, 1834, at Kirtland; she died in January 1841. He was appointed a bishop at Nauvoo in 1841. He married Levira Clark on May 30, 1841, in Scott County, Illinois. Samuel died July 30, 1844, at Nauvoo.

Source: Samuel Harrison Smith, *josephsmithpapers.org*

Photo courtesy The Church of Jesus Christ of Latter-day Saints

Five Secret Questions

It was the late summer of 1831 when two missionaries traveling through Illinois stopped in the small town of Paris to preach. One of those missionaries was particularly interesting, as he testified of witnessing an angel and of actually seeing the plates of the Book of Mormon. A young schoolteacher named William heard what the missionaries had to say and was convinced that it was true.

As the missionaries moved on, William closed his school and went after them. Along the way, he devoured the Book of Mormon and even interviewed men listed in the book as witnesses. Finally, William declared, "I was bound as an honest man to acknowledge the truth and validity of the Book of Mormon, and that I had found the people of the Lord."

With that, William was baptized.

On October 25, 1831, William first met Joseph Smith—and, as so many others had done before him, he asked Joseph for a revelation on his behalf. Joseph inquired of the Lord for William, and a revelation did come. William wrote it down as Joseph dictated it. He said that the revelation brought great comfort to his heart "because it answered many questions which had been on my mind with uncertainty and anxiety."

Only later do we see the miraculous significance of that revelation. William told of putting five questions to the Lord in secret. If Joseph addressed those questions, thought William, it would be a sign that Joseph was indeed a prophet. The result? William said, "I now testify in the fear of God, that every question which I had thus lodged in the ears of the Lord of Sabbath were answered to my full and entire satisfaction, I desire it for a testimony of Joseph's inspiration. And I to this day consider it to me an evidence which I cannot refute."

That revelation answering the five secret questions is known today as Doctrine and Covenants 66, and that young schoolteacher was William E. McLellin.

Perhaps what is most compelling about this story is what happened after the revelation was received. By 1838, William E. McLellin was an embittered enemy of Joseph Smith and the Latter-day Saints. It was he who asked permission to flog the Prophet when Joseph was imprisoned in Liberty Jail. It was he who, along with others, ransacked the home of Emma Smith, stealing such valuables as a horse and saddle.

McLellin left the Church, never to return. And yet to his dying day, McLellin affirmed the truthfulness of the Book of Mormon and the validity of that revelation dictated by Joseph Smith—considering it, he said, as "evidence" of Joseph's prophetic calling "which I cannot refute."

Source: William E. McLellin, 1806–1883, *boap.org*

98

William E. McLellin was born January 18, 1806, at Smith County, Tennessee. A schoolteacher, physician, and publisher, he married Cynthia Ann on July 30, 1829; she died by the summer of 1831. William was baptized a member of The Church of Jesus Christ of Latter-day Saints by Hyrum Smith on August 20, 1831, in Jackson County, Missouri, and was ordained an elder by Hyrum Smith and Edward Partridge on August 24, 1831. William was ordained a high priest by Oliver Cowdery on October 25, 1831. He married Emeline Miller on April 26, 1832, at Portage County, Ohio. William was ordained a member of the Quorum of the Twelve on February 15, 1835, but was disfellowshipped over difficulties arising while he was serving an eastern mission with members of the Quorum of the Twelve; he was reinstated September 26, 1835. William wrote a letter of withdrawal from the Church in August 1836. He was again sustained to the Quorum of the Twelve on September 3, 1837, at Kirtland. William was excommunicated in 1838 and broke with all organized religion in 1869. He died March 14, 1883, at Independence.

Source: William Earl McLellin, *josephsmithpapers.org*

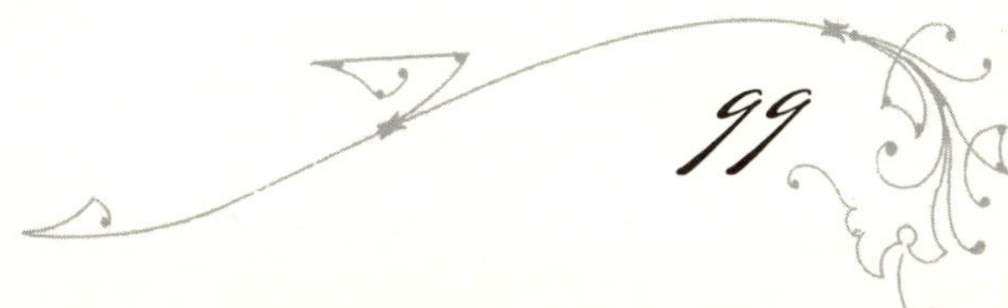

Mary Elizabeth Rollins

Photo courtesy The Church of Jesus Christ of Latter-day Saints

Joseph Smith and the Spirit of Revelation

What was it like to be there and witness Joseph Smith receiving revelations? Brigham Young was a witness, and he said:

> Those who were acquainted with [the Prophet Joseph] knew when the Spirit of revelation was upon him, for his countenance wore an expression peculiar to himself while under that influence. He preached by the Spirit of revelation, and taught in his council by it, and those who were acquainted with him could discover it at once, for at such times there was a peculiar clearness and transparency in his face. (*Journal of Discourses*, 9:89)

Mary Elizabeth Rollins was just a girl when she witnessed the Prophet receiving revelation. She left this description of events in February 1831:

Joseph got up and began to speak to us. As he began to speak very solemnly and very earnestly, all at once his countenance changed and he stood mute. Those who looked at him that day said there was a search light within him, over every part of his body. I never saw anything like it on the earth. I could not take my eyes off him; he got so white that anyone who saw him would have thought he was transparent. I remember I thought I could almost see the cheek bones through the flesh. I have been through many changes since but that is photographed on my brain. I shall remember it and see in my mind's eye as long as I remain upon the earth.

He stood some moments. He looked over the congregation as if to pierce every heart. He said, "Do you know who has been in your midst?"

One of the Smiths said an angel of the Lord.

Martin Harris said, "It was our Lord and Savior, Jesus Christ."

Joseph put his hand down on Martin and said: "God revealed that to you. Brethren and sisters, the Spirit of God has been here. The Savior has been in your midst this night and I want you to remember it. There is a veil over your eyes for you could not endure to look upon Him. You must be fed with milk, not with strong meat. I want you to remember this as if it were the last thing that escaped my lips. He has given all of you to me and has sealed you up to everlasting life that where he is, you may be also. And if you are tempted of Satan say, 'Get behind me, Satan.'"

These words are figured upon my brain and I never took my eye off his countenance. Then he knelt down and prayed. I have never heard anything like it before or since. I felt that he was talking to the Lord and that power rested down upon the congregation. Every soul felt it. The spirit rested upon us in every fiber of our bodies, and we received a sermon from the lips of the representative of God.

How blessed we are to have the accounts of those who witnessed for themselves Joseph Smith receiving revelations such as those found in the Doctrine and Covenants.

Sources: *Journal of Discourses*, 9:89

"The Testimony of Mary Elizabeth Rollins Lightner," 1905, BYU Archives and Manuscripts, *ldshistory.us*

Mary Elizabeth Rollins was born April 9, 1818, in Lima, Ontario County, New York, and moved to Kirtland, Geauga County, Ohio, ca. 1828. A seamstress, schoolteacher, and hotelier, Mary Elizabeth was baptized a member of The Church of Jesus Christ of Latter-day Saints in October 1830 in Kirtland. She married Adam Lightner on August 11, 1835, and became the plural wife of Joseph Smith when she was sealed to him in February 1842. Mary Elizabeth joined the Female Relief Society of Nauvoo on April 14, 1842. She migrated to Minersville, Beaver County, Utah Territory, arriving September 20, 1863, and served as the president of the Relief Society there in about 1869. Mary Elizabeth died December 17, 1913, in Minersville.

Source: Mary Elizabeth Rollins Lightner, *josephsmithpapers.org*

The Matriarch of the Gathering

Mother Polly Peck Knight and her family first met young Joseph Smith in the fall of 1826. While he was struggling to survive and preparing himself to receive the golden plates, the Knights were well-established landowners and farmers. The Knights would later befriend Joseph and help support him while he translated the Book of Mormon.

The Knights were there on April 6, 1830, when the Church was organized in Fayette, New York. On June 28, 1830, Mother Knight was baptized, along with others of her family. Her large extended family became the first branch in this dispensation of the new Church of Christ, and because of their numbers they drew intense persecution—more so, perhaps, than any other group in that period of Church history. It was difficult for them, and Joseph spent considerable time among them teaching and ministering.

Then in December 1830 came a startling revelation. The Church was to "assemble together at the Ohio" (D&C 37:3). The entire Church was moving. A succeeding revelation declared, "They that have farms that cannot be sold, let them be left or rented as seemeth them good" (D&C 38:37). Obedient to that revelation, the Knights left the farm they had lived on since 1811. Part of it had still not been sold when they set out for Ohio.

The Knights arrived in Ohio in May 1831, and after consecrating all they owned, they were given land to begin anew on the farm of Leman Copley in Thompson, Ohio. They set to with a vigor plowing, planting, fencing, and building homes. And then three weeks later, Copley, now angry and disaffected from Mormonism, ordered them off his land.

Once again, Polly and her family and friends of the Colesville Branch were homeless. Then came another revelation inviting them to be the first to know the location of Zion, gather and purchase its land, and establish the foundations of its city.

It was July 25, 1831, when the Colesville Saints arrived in Independence, Missouri. The trip was particularly difficult for Mother Polly Peck Knight. She grew weaker and weaker as they journeyed. At one point, her son Newel left the company to obtain wood to build a coffin for her.

Yet she hung on, determined to make it to Zion and praying that she would.

And she did.

She was able to participate in laying the foundation of Zion, and in the dedication ceremonies both of the land and its temple. No sooner was that complete than on August 6, 1831, she "quietly fell asleep rejoicing in the everlasting gospel and praising God that she was able to see the land of Zion." Her greatest desire had been fulfilled.

Mother Polly Peck Knight gave her all in faith and journeyed 1,300 miles to reach the promised land—the same distance that thousands would later travel from Nauvoo to Salt Lake. And there she lies, "a worthy member asleep in Jesus until the resurrection." She died just on the west side of the Big Blue River west of Independence, Missouri, becoming, as it were, the matriarch of the gathering—the first of thousands to sacrifice all and die on the journey to Zion.

Source: History of the Saints Interview with William G. Hartley, February 2014

Polly Peck, the daughter of Joseph Peck and Elizabeth Read, was born April 16, 1774, in Guilford, Cumberland County, New York. She later lived in Windham County, Vermont, where she married Joseph Knight Sr. in 1795. She was baptized a member of The Church of Jesus Christ of Latter-day Saints by Oliver Cowdery on June 28, 1830, at Colesville. Polly moved with the Colesville Branch to Thompson, Geauga County, Ohio, in April–May 1831 and to Kaw Township, Jackson County, Missouri, in July 1831. She died August 7, 1831, in Kaw Township.

Source: Polly Peck Knight, *josephsmithpapers.org*

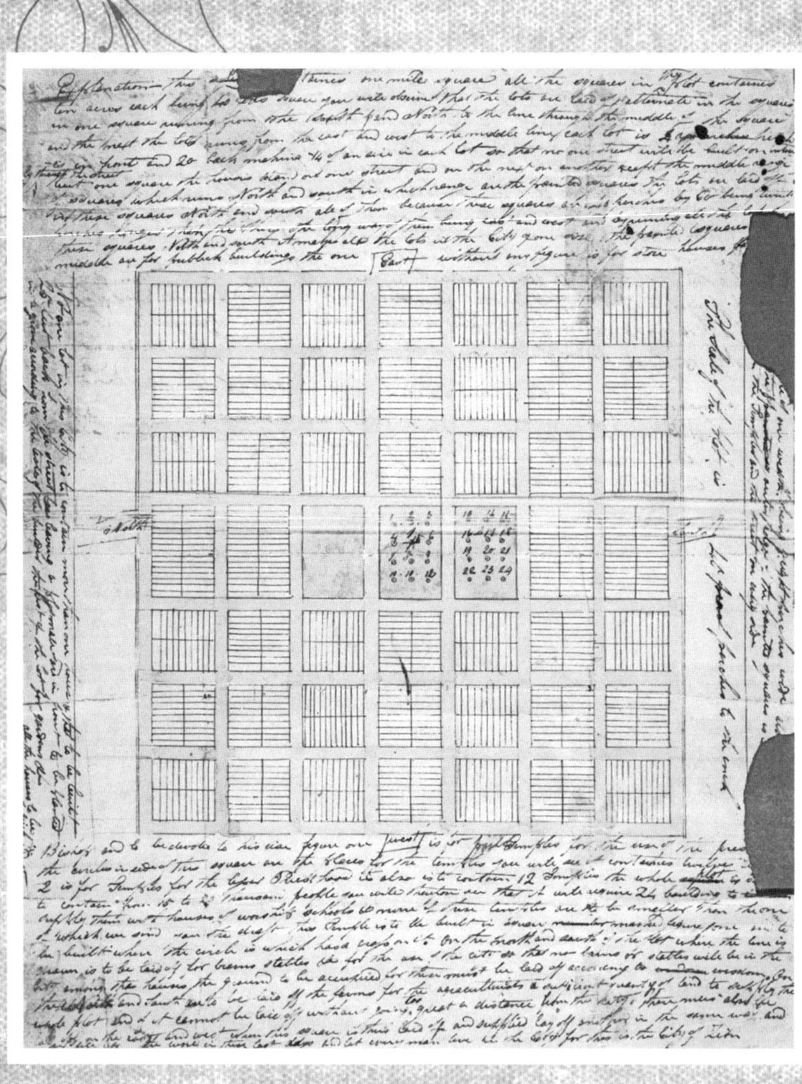

The Plat of Zion showing the temple as the central location of the community, near Independence, Missouri, 1833

Photo courtesy The Church of Jesus Christ of Latter-day Saints

Purchasing Zion

I saiah spoke often and eloquently about the Zion that would be established in the last days. Prophets looked forward to it and rejoiced in their knowledge of it. Among them, Ether prophesied that in the last days "a new Jerusalem should be built up upon this land, unto the remnant of the seed of Joseph" (Ether 13:6).

It was April 5, 1829, when a revelation commanded young Oliver Cowdery to "seek to bring forth and establish the cause of Zion" (D&C 6:6). That command would be echoed again and again, and Joseph Smith would be charged and inspired by the Almighty "to move the cause of Zion in mighty power for good" (D&C 21:7).

Among the Saints, excitement began to mount as understanding grew of what Zion was and would be . It was to be, as Joseph learned, both a people and a place.

Enoch built the first city of Zion—a people of one heart and one mind in righteousness, with no poor among them (see Moses 7:18). In time these people walked with God, and He dwelt in the midst of Zion until that day when they were taken from the earth

with a promise that someday the City of Zion in heaven would come back to earth to greet the City of Zion—the New Jerusalem—established here.

Joseph and the Saints knew this city was to be built, and they knew they were to do it, but where and when was that to happen? Can you imagine the sense of honor and purpose that infused those first Saints—to be charged with fulfilling that prophecy, to establish the perfect society of Enoch once more?

They soon learned that as time marched forward, Zion would "be the only people that shall not be at war one with another" (D&C 45:70). They also learned that Zion had to be established as a place of refuge and safety in preparation for the Lord's Second Coming. All depended on it.

Anticipation mounted when the Saints learned that the new City of Zion was somewhere on the western frontier in the land of Missouri. On June 6, 1831, a number of people were called to go to Missouri, and there the Lord promised He would make known the location of Zion (see D&C 52:5).

On July 20, 1831, as Joseph and his friends stood near Independence, Jackson County, Missouri, the Lord revealed, "This is the land of promise, and the place for the City of Zion" (D&C 57:2,) and "the place which is now called Independence is the center place; and a spot for the temple is lying westward, upon a lot which is not far from courthouse" (D&C 57:3).

On August 2, 1831, the land of Zion was dedicated, and on August 3, 1831, the Prophet Joseph dedicated the temple site. Then came the practical command of the Almighty: "Behold it is wisdom that the land should be purchased by the saints . . . that they might obtain it for an everlasting inheritance" (D&C 57:4–5). Subsequently they began to purchase Zion with donated monies.

In that first year of 1831, Bishop Edward Partridge expended about $1,200 in buying tracts of land where the Saints could settle and build their city of hope. And who was the first principal donor—the man who, at the Lord's command, laid $1,200 at the feet of Bishop Partridge and paid for the foundations of Zion? Martin Harris—the same man who paid for the printing of the Book of Mormon.

Source: History of the Saints Interview with Alexander L. Baugh, October 2014

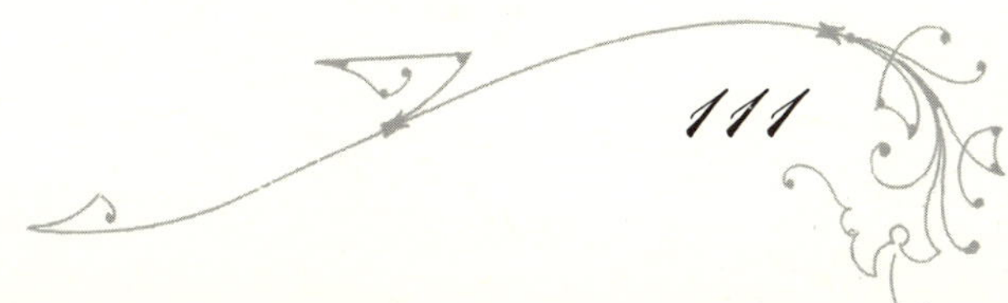

In June 1831, the fourth conference of the Church
was held in a small log schoolhouse located on a hill
overlooking the Isaac Morley farm; art by Kelly Donavan

The Man of Sin Was Revealed

On June 4, 1831, some sixty-two men assembled for a conference as commended by revelation in a little log schoolhouse on the Morley Farm just out of Kirtland, Ohio. They came with high expectation, as a previous revelation from the Lord had promised that His Spirit would be poured out upon them. They came expecting a Pentecostal experience.

Joseph Smith opened the meeting and began to preach. According to John Whitmer, "The Spirit of the Lord fell upon Joseph in an unusual manner."

Joseph then prophesied "that John the Revelator was then among the ten tribes of Israel . . . to prepare them for their return." He further declared that the elders would depart at the close of the conference to begin their missionary labors.

Then Joseph looked at Lyman Wight and promised him that he would see the Lord in that meeting. Joseph laid his hands on Elder Wight and ordained him to the high priesthood—as we would say, Joseph ordained Elder Wight a high priest. Joseph proceeded to ordain others and then called on Lyman to speak.

Lyman Wight stepped up and manifested that he saw the Savior. At Joseph's direction, Lyman began ordaining others to the same office. Joseph did the same.

Suddenly a different spirit seemed to manifest itself. Two men, Harvey Whitlock and John Murdock, seemed bound by some force that acted on their bodies or speech. Joseph inquired of the Lord then stepped forward and, laying his hands on Harvey's head, cast out the evil spirit.

The evil spirit then entered Leman Copley, who was standing at the window outside the cabin. Copley tipped forward, did a complete somersault, and came down on his back across some benches. He was quickly administered to. The evil spirit then possessed another man, who fell to the floor and screamed like a panther. And on it went the rest of the day and into the evening, the forces of evil seizing those in attendance and the men of the priesthood rescuing each in turn.

Indeed, as had been prophesied by Paul, the man of sin was revealed on that day.

While some may cringe at the telling of this story, the men who were there counted the day's events a great blessing, for now they understood for themselves the spirit of the evil one. Before this event, they could not discern the difference between a good spirit and a bad one—now they knew. That day saw not only the first ordinations to the office of high priest in this dispensation, but it was also a turning point in the spiritual maturity of the young church.

Sources: Minutes, circa 3–4 June 1831, "General Conference" of the Church of Christ in Kirtland, Ohio, Historical Introduction, *josephsmithpapers.org*

Mark Lyman Staker, *Hearken O Ye People: The Historical Setting of Joseph Smith's Ohio Revelations* (Draper, Utah: Greg Kofford Books, 2010), 156–161

"They Will Return"

When two missionaries came into the small New Hampshire community of Lyman, they encountered a nineteen-year-old man who had been searching earnestly for the truth. Upon hearing the sure testimony of Elders Orson Pratt and Lyman E. Johnson, he was converted and baptized April 27, 1832. Upon his baptism, Amasa Mason Lyman was immediately rejected by his family.

Amasa determined to join the Saints in Ohio some seven hundred miles away, his greatest desire being to meet Joseph Smith. That desire was fulfilled on July 1, 1832, when Amasa Mason Lyman first met the Prophet Joseph Smith. As they shook hands for the first time, Amasa later recalled, "I felt as one of old in the presence of the Lord. My strength seemed to be gone, so that it required an effort on my part to stand on my feet . . . and the still small voice of the Spirit whispered its testimony in the depths of my soul, where it has ever remained that he, Joseph Smith, was a man of God."

Shortly after meeting the Prophet, Amasa was called as a missionary—again and again he was called, serving ten missions in ten years. He was a member of Zion's Camp, and later he was one of those standing with Joseph when a Missouri militia general ordered them all to be taken to the public square and shot the next morning.

After much devoted service, Amasa was called as an Apostle and as a counselor to the Prophet Joseph Smith in Nauvoo. Upon Joseph's death, it was Amasa who stood with Brigham Young and the Twelve and influenced the Saints to do likewise.

Amasa was a full participant in the events of the Great Mormon Exodus of Nauvoo in 1846 and the subsequent colonization of the West, but in the 1860s the problems began.

Inexplicably, the man who had been so valiant and devoted began to teach strange doctrines and to manifest an attitude of rebellion. His brethren were patient and attempted reconciliation, but when Amasa would not relent, he was finally excommunicated from the Church in 1870. He died February 4, 1877, in Fillmore, Utah, not a member of the Church.

As mortals tend to judge matters, Amasa's story was a terrible tragedy. He had done so much good, and after all of that to stumble at the end. . . .

But the story does not end there. There is more. Sometime in 1908, one of Amasa's daughters had a dream in which she saw her father, dressed in black, standing across the wide gulf of a river. Martha tried to go to him, but she could not. He told her he was tired of wearing black, that he missed his family, and then he said, "Go tell Francis. He's the only one who can help me." Francis was Amasa's son and the President of the Quorum of the Twelve Apostles.

When this dream was related to Church President Joseph F. Smith, he said, "It sounds to me like your father has suffered long enough. We'll see what we can do." Subsequently, on January 12, 1909, Francis Marion Lyman was baptized by proxy on behalf of his father, and President Joseph F. Smith laid his hands upon Francis, confirmed Amasa a member of the Church, and restored all Amasa's former blessings—his priesthood, his apostleship, his sealings.

It was Elder Orson F. Whitney who wrote, "Though some of the sheep may wander, the eye of the Shepherd is upon them, and sooner or later they will feel the tentacles of Divine Providence reaching out after them and drawing them back to the fold. Either in this life or the life to come, they will return. They will have to pay their debt to justice; they will suffer for their sins; and may tread a thorny path; but if it leads them at last, like the penitent Prodigal, to a loving and forgiving father's heart and home, the painful experience will not have been in vain."

Source: History of the Saints, *Amasa Mason Lyman: A Labor of Love,* 2013

Amasa Mason Lyman, the son of Boswell Lyman and Martha Mason, was born March 30, 1813, at Lyman, Grafton County, New Hampshire. A boatman, gunsmith, and farmer, he was baptized a member of The Church of Jesus Christ of Latter-day Saints by Lyman E. Johnson on April 27, 1832. Amasa moved to Hiram, Portage County, Ohio, in May–June 1832, and was there ordained an elder by Joseph Smith and Frederick G. Williams on August 23, 1832. A counselor in the First Presidency in 1843–1844, he was admitted to the Council of Fifty on March 26, 1844. Amasa moved to Fillmore, Millard County, Utah Territory, in 1863. He was deprived of his apostleship on May 6, 1867, and was excommunicated on May 12, 1870. He became president of the Godbeite Church of Zion in 1870. Amasa died February 4, 1877, at Fillmore.

Source: Amasa Mason Lyman, *josephsmithpapers.org*

The Conversion of Brigham Young

They were a typical large New England family: very poor—so poor, in fact, that the children were not afforded the luxury of an education. The only learning they received came in the form of hard work on the farm.

The parents were "some of the most strict religionists upon the earth." To violate the family's religious standards would bring forth swift paternal discipline. Mother was of a more gentle approach and revered by her children. She encouraged them to "do everything that is good; do nothing that is evil; and if you see any persons in distress administer to their wants."

But then tuberculosis claimed that mother, Nabby Young, resulting in the family being broken up and scattered. At the young age of sixteen, Nabby and John Young's ninth son, Brigham, left home to make his way in the world.

About this time, Brigham's brother Lorenzo had a dream in which he saw a gold carriage drawn by a beautiful pair of white horses. The Savior was in the carriage. When it stopped before Lorenzo, "the Savior inquired, 'Where is your brother Brigham?'

After answering his question He inquired about my other brothers, and concerning my father. . . . He stated that he wanted us all, but especially my brother Brigham."

Brigham matured and became a skilled and conscientious craftsman. When he was twenty-three, he married Miriam Works, who was described as a "beautiful blond with blue eyes and wavy hair; gentle and lovable." Together they had two children, Elizabeth and Vilate.

Brigham Young was fiercely independent. Though he never drank, when members of his family urged him to sign a temperance pledge, he refused, saying, "I wish to do just right, without being bound to do it; I want my liberty. My independence is sacred to me."

Brigham's independence carried into religion as he developed his own ideas of God and the scriptures. Amidst the fervor of revivalism, he remained skeptical of the churches available to him. They seemed empty. He wanted to know God and know how to find Him, but none could answer his questions. Angry ministers called him an infidel.

It was September 1827 when Brigham saw a marvelous vision in the heavens of warring armies. He would remember that vision all his days and considered it a sign. Yet Brigham became discouraged. His questions remained unanswered—his quest unfulfilled.

Then the Book of Mormon came into the family. Father, brothers, sisters, and relatives all embraced it quickly, but not Brigham. He was leery of being taken in. For eighteen months he pondered the book, compared its teachings to the Bible, and scrutinized those who believed in it.

It was not enough to feel or believe it was true; he had to know.

Then came the day when Eleazer Miller bore humble testimony to the truth of the Restoration, and Brigham's soul was filled with light and certainty. He was baptized April 14, 1832. His wife, Miriam, followed three weeks later.

Brigham was reborn. "I wanted to thunder and roar out the Gospel to the nations," he said, "It burned in my bones like fire pent up." And preach the gospel he did, but he could never go far from home. Miriam had contracted tuberculosis and was slipping away. Each day Brigham

> got breakfast for his wife, himself, and the little girls, dressed the children, cleaned up the house, carried his wife to the rocking chair by the fireplace and left her there until he could return in the evening. When he came home he cooked his own and the family's supper, put his wife back to bed and finished up the day's domestic labors.

In September 1832, Miriam Young passed away, she and Brigham confident they would be together again forever. With his wife gone and his daughters under the motherly watch-care of Vilate Kimball, Brigham Young closed his shop, gave away his earthly possessions, and set out to preach that gospel that seemed like a fire in his bones.

Source: Ronald K. Esplin, "Conversion and Transformation: Brigham Young's New York Roots and the Search for Bible Religion," *Regional Studies in Latter-day Saint Church History*, 1992, 165–201

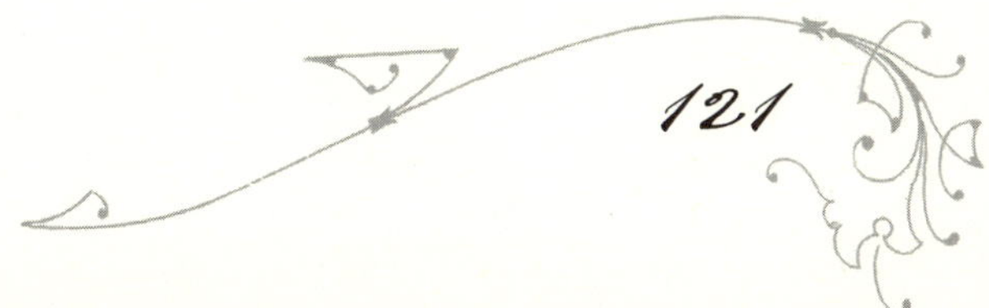

121

Brigham Young, the son of John Young and Abigail (Nabby) Howe, was born June 1, 1801, at Whitingham, Windham County, Vermont. A carpenter, painter, glazier, and colonizer, he was brought up in a Methodist household and later joined the Methodist Church. He married Miriam Angeline Works of Aurelius, Cayuga County, New York, on October 8, 1824. He was living at Mendon, Monroe County, New York, when he was baptized a member of The Church of Jesus Christ of Latter-day Saints by Eleazer Miller on April 9/15, 1832. Miriam died September 8, 1832, and Brigham married Mary Ann Angell on March 31, 1834, in Geauga County. He was ordained a member of the Quorum of the Twelve by Oliver Cowdery, David Whitmer, and Martin Harris on February 14, 1835, at Kirtland. He was appointed president of the Quorum of the Twelve on April 14, 1840. Brigham participated in

Photo courtesy The Church of Jesus Christ of Latter-day Saints

plural marriage during Joseph Smith's lifetime. After Joseph Smith's death, he was sustained with the Twelve to administer the affairs of the Church on August 8, 1844, at Nauvoo. Recognized as "President of the whole Church of Latter Day Saints" at a conference in Nauvoo on April 7, 1845, Brigham directed Latter-day Saint migration from Nauvoo to the Salt Lake Valley in 1846–1848. He reorganized the First Presidency of the Church in December 1847. He served as governor of Utah Territory in 1850–1857 and directed establishment of hundreds of settlements in the western United States. Brigham died August 29, 1877, at Salt Lake City.

Source: Brigham Young, *josephsmithpapers.org*

Tar and Feathers

It was sometime in the wee hours of the morning of March 25, 1832, when an infuriated mob exploded through the door of the summer kitchen of the John Johnson home in Hiram, Ohio. They pounced on twenty-six-year-old Joseph Smith Jr. and began carrying him out the door.

It all happened so quickly that Joseph was on the stoop before he came awake. Struggling, he freed one leg and kicked one of the mobbers in the face, sending him sprawling. The man jumped to his feet and with his hands covered in his own blood, he grabbed Joseph by the throat and choked him until he lost consciousness.

When Joseph revived, he saw his friend and counselor Sidney Rigdon stretched out unmoving on the cold ground. Supposing that Sidney was dead, Joseph asked the mob for mercy.

"Call on yer God for help," they responded. "We'll show you no mercy!"

Men seemed to come from everywhere and join the fray. They argued about whether to kill Joseph or just rough him up. The decision was made to hurt him, and to that end they proceeded. Tearing off all his clothes but his shirt collar, they beat, kicked,

and scratched him. One man fell on Joseph like a mad cat and scratched his body with his nails, crying as he did, "That's the way the Holy Ghost falls on folks."

Someone brought a bucket of hot tar that they then smeared over Joseph's lacerated body, at the same time trying to force the tar paddle into his mouth. He resisted. They then tried to force into his mouth a vial of poison—aquafortis, or nitric acid. Again he clenched his jaw and fought back. Had they succeeded, the poison would have burned his throat, ruined his voice, and probably killed him. As it was, they succeeded only in knocking out one of his teeth and spilling the acid over his skin, severely burning him.

How bad was this attack? They tore out a patch of his hair by the roots that never grew back. They injured his side in such a way that it pained him the rest of his life. But that's not all: they killed him. Joseph would later describe standing above his body and watching as the mob beat him and poured the acid over his face and neck.

Then a noise was heard, and the mob fled in fear, leaving Joseph on the ground. Slowly, he regained consciousness. He tried to sit up but couldn't. Unable to breathe, he pulled the tar from his mouth. After a time, he made his way home.

Emma stood in the doorway and fainted at the sight of him. Joseph asked for a blanket for cover and went inside by the fire. His friends spent the night peeling and scraping the tar from his body, sometimes taking off layers of skin with it.

The incident made a lasting impression on mobbers and members alike when the next morning, the Sabbath, Joseph stood and meekly preached a sermon, after which he baptized three people. About a week later, in obedience to revelation, Joseph set out for an extended visit to Missouri. He simply would not give up.

Why the mob? What was it that had so infuriated the locals that ministers, doctors, and former friends joined a mob to kill Joseph, or at least silence him? There were many reasons, chief among them a new revelation Joseph and Sidney had received the month before about the three degrees of glory, which we know as Doctrine and Covenants 76.

Light and truth stir up darkness. It has ever been that way, and it still is.

Source: History of the Saints Interview with Mark Lyman Staker, November 2014

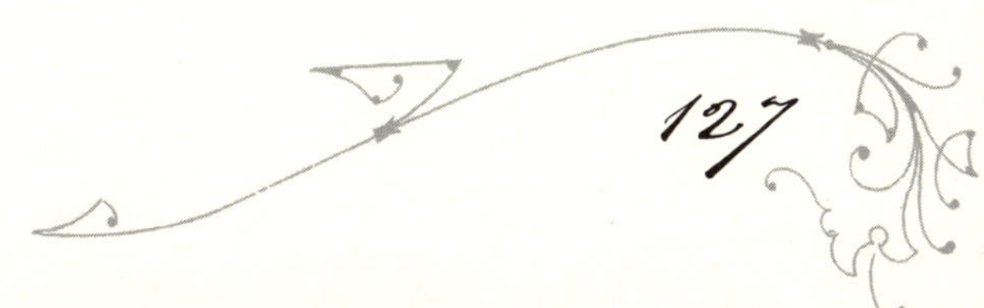

Translation Room, John Johnson Home, Hiram, Ohio;
courtesy Mormon Historic Sites Foundation

The Vision

It is an established truth verified by thousands of witnesses that the Lord Jesus Christ rose from the tomb on Resurrection morning with a glorified and perfected body of flesh and bones. Through these ancient testimonies we find our faith and hope. This is the story, last of all, of another witness of the Risen Christ found in the Doctrine and Covenants, another volume that witnesses of the Lord Jesus Christ, that He lives and still speaks to men.

Joseph Smith and his family were living in the home of John and Elsa Johnson in Hiram, Ohio. On Thursday, February 16, 1832, the day was cold, with temperatures near twenty degrees and nearly three feet of snow on the ground. Upstairs in the southeast corner of the home, Joseph and his scribe, Sidney Rigdon, were translating the holy scriptures. They came to John 5:28–29, which quotes the Savior saying, "Marvel not at this: for the hour is coming, in the which all that are in the graves shall hear his voice, And shall come forth; they who have done good unto the resurrection of life; and they who have done evil, unto the resurrection of damnation."

The passage caused them to marvel. There was a current debate among the religionists of the day. Did the next world consist of only heaven and hell, or were there three different rewards as some were teaching?

As Joseph and Sidney meditated on the subject, the Lord touched the eyes of their understanding; they were opened, and the glory of the Lord shone round about. And that began a series of visions that lasted for hours.

There may have been as many as twelve men in that room with them who saw the glory but not the vision. No one moved or spoke as Joseph and Sidney gazed up into heaven and described what they saw. One witness, Philo Dibble, said, "Joseph wore black clothes, but at this time seemed to be dressed in an element of glorious white, and his face shone as if it were transparent. . . . [He] sat firmly and calmly all the time in the midst of a magnificent glory, but Sidney sat limp and pale, apparently as limber as a rag."

Joseph and Sidney saw many things, only a hundredth part of which they would ever share.

That vision would clarify as no other revelation did what glories and blessings would be bestowed upon men by the redemption and resurrection of Jesus Christ. The significance of the first vision they saw that day stands today in remarkable power:

> We beheld the glory of the Son on the right
> hand of the Father and received of his fulness . . .
> And now, after the many testimonies which
> have been given of him, this is the testimony, last
> of all, which we give of him: That he lives!

For we saw Him, even on the right hand of
God; and we heard the voice bearing record that
he is the Only Begotten of the Father—

That by him, and through him, and of him,
the worlds are and were created, and the inhabitants thereof are begotten sons and daughters
unto God. (D&C 76:20–24)

Source: History of the Saints Interview with Mark Lyman Staker,
November 2014

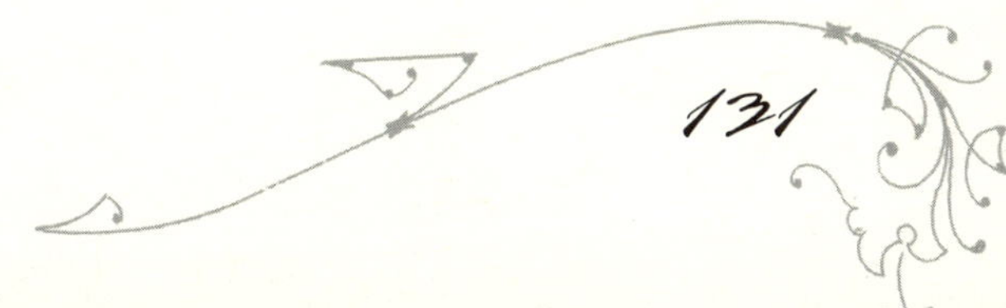

131

Photo courtesy The Church of Jesus Christ of Latter-day Saints

"I Bore My Abuse"

The love God has for us is called *charity*, and if we don't have it, we are nothing. With it, however, we are fit subjects for heaven. This story powerfully illustrates one reason why charity is the greatest virtue of them all.

On July 20, 1833, in Independence, Missouri, a mob of some four to five hundred men angrily decided that they did not like the Latter-day Saints who had taken residence in their county—and they declared that the Saints must leave. They drafted a resolution to that effect over the signature of the leading citizens of the county. Twelve men were appointed to present the demands to the Latter-day Saint leaders. They approached Edward Partridge, William W. Phelps, and others with the unjust demands.

The men asked for three months to consider the mob's demands and decide a course. Their request was denied. They asked for ten days. That too was denied. They had fifteen minutes to decide what to do with 1,200 people and their possessions.

133

Meanwhile, the mob returned to the courthouse and awaited their decision. When it did not come quickly enough, the mob attacked. They went first to the Church-owned printing office, kicked open the door, tossed out the press, and tore down the entire building, burying in the process two of the Phelps children. They then went for the Church-owned Gilbert and Whitney Store and began demolishing it and scattering the goods. Only when Gilbert promised to be out in three days did the mob desist in their actions.

With loud yelling and cursing, the mob began searching for the Church leaders. They burst into the home of Edward Partridge and, while his family watched, they dragged him to the public square of Independence. With the mob frothing around them, Edward Partridge and young Charles Allen were given an ultimatum: they must renounce the Book of Mormon and Joseph Smith or leave the county.

Bishop Partridge refused to do either, stating he "was not conscious of having injured anyone in the county, therefore," he said, "I could not consent to leave it."

This infuriated the mob further, and they began to strip him of his clothes for the intent of tarring and feathering him. He asked

134

for the dignity of keeping his shirt and pants on, a request that was granted. The mob poured hot tar mixed with pearl ash—a flesh-eating acid—over his body and then covered him with feathers. Partridge stood there without struggle or retaliation as they brutalized him.

"I bore my abuse," he later said, "with so much resignation and meekness that it appeared to astound the multitude who permitted me to retire in silence, many looking very solemn. Their sympathies having been touched as I thought. And as to myself I was so filled with the spirit and love of God that I had no hatred toward my persecutors or anyone else."

There it is! Charity is a gift from God through the Holy Ghost, and when a man is filled with the love of God, he bears no ill will to any man—not even, and especially, his enemies. That is why charity is the greatest of all. Thank goodness that only people like this dwell with God.

As for the good bishop, he would go on to offer himself a ransom for his beleaguered people, and he eventually so wore out his life that he died a premature death in Nauvoo.

Source: History of the Saints, *Edward Partridge: One of the Lord's Great Men* (DVD), 2017

Edward Partridge, the son of William Partridge and Jemima Bidwell, was born August 27, 1793, at Pittsfield, Berkshire County, Massachusetts. He married Lydia Clisbee on August

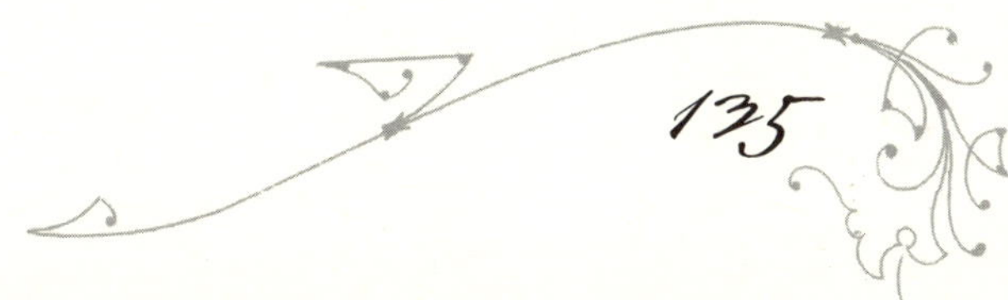

125

22, 1819, at Painesville. He was baptized a member of The Church of Jesus Christ of Latter-day Saints by Joseph Smith on December 11, 1830, in the nearby Seneca River. Edward accompanied Joseph Smith to Independence, Jackson County, Missouri, and was appointed to oversee settlement of the Saints in Missouri during the summer of 1831. Edward was tarred and feathered during mob violence in Jackson County, Missouri, in July 1833, and he fled with his family to Clay County, Missouri, in November 1833. In the fall of 1836, Edward was forced to move from Clay County to what soon became Caldwell County, Missouri, where he continued to serve as bishop. Jailed at Richmond, Ray County, Missouri, in the fall of 1838, he was expelled from the state in 1839. Edward was appointed bishop of Upper Ward at Commerce (later Nauvoo), Hancock County, Illinois, in 1839. He died May 27, 1840, at Nauvoo.

Source: Edward Partridge, *josephsmithpapers.org*

"A Day Long to Be Remembered"

In the Spring of 1846, the Latter-day Saints were an exiled people in a wilderness. Their leaders were ahead of them on the prairies of Iowa, seeking a new home somewhere in the West. The first company of Saints left Nauvoo in a tightly organized group, following Brigham Young and the Twelve for a place "where none could hurt or make afraid." The rest of the Saints, desperate not to be left behind, departed haphazardly, doing the best they could. Among those was Lucius Scoville and his family.

Lucius had once owned a bakery in Nauvoo, but now he too was preparing to take his family "into the wilderness." Then May 6, 1846, just a week before his preparations were finished, the unthinkable happened: Lucius received a call to go to England as a missionary. How could he accept such a call? How could he go to England and leave his family to find their own way across more than a thousand miles of wilderness?

He determined he could not.

On May 14, 1846, Lucius crossed the Mississippi River with his family and began the long trek west to a new home, not knowing beforehand where they would settle. Over the next two weeks they journeyed slowly across Iowa, a handful among Latter-day Saint refugees scattered as far as the eye could see in all directions.

Then, on May 30, 1846, "a day long to be remembered" as Lucius recorded it in his journal, three men came into camp from the west just as the family was eating breakfast. The men were going back to Nauvoo. Lucius felt that familiar pull and knew his duty. He "resolved then and there to start on [his] mission to England." It was "a painful duty," he wrote, "to leave my family to go into the wilderness, and I turn and go the other way." Nonetheless, Lucius was determined to fill his mission, he said, "if it cost me all that I had on this earth."

Of that day, Lucius wrote:

> Never since I have been in this Church have I seen anything in comparison to this trial. To think of leaving my wife and children to go into the wilderness without my being with them to look after them, and they weeping to think of my leaving them and going to a far distant country, but I left them bidding them God speed. By this time, I was completely overcome by my feelings and could not keep from bursting into a flood of tears, and thus I left them and started on my mission for England.

Lucius took leave of his family without purse or scrip and undertook a journey of some six thousand miles to England. As he journeyed across the Atlantic, his wife and children followed the Brethren in faith to the West.

The Lord's admonition seems particularly applicable to Lucius Scoville and the sacrifice made by him and his family: "let every man learn his duty and act in the office in which he is appointed" (D&C 107:99).

Source: Journal of Lucius N. Scoville, LDS Church Archives

Lucius Scoville, the son of Joel Scovil and Lydia, was born March 18, 1806, in Middlebury, New Haven County, Connecticut. A farmer, baker, and clerk, Lucius was baptized a member of The Church of Jesus Christ of Latter-day Saints by Joseph Smith on July 2, 1836. He moved to Nauvoo, Hancock County, Illinois, by 1841 and served a mission to England in 1846–1847. Lucius returned to the United States on August 10, 1847, and was appointed Church immigration agent in New Orleans. He arrived in the Salt Lake Valley in October 1850 and moved to Provo, Utah County, Utah Territory, by August 1852. Lucius moved to Springville, Utah County, by 1880, and he died there on February 14, 1889.

Photo courtesy The Church of Jesus Christ of Latter-day Saints

Large in Spirit, Not Just Stature

Standing nearly seven feet tall and weighing close to three hundred pounds, Freeman Nickerson of Perrysburg, New York, was not just large in stature but also large in spirit.

In April 1833, Freeman joined the Latter-day Saints along with his wife, Huldah, and some of his nine children. The fire burned hot for Freeman, and his greatest desire was to share the gospel, starting with his family.

Two of Freeman's sons, Moses and Freeman, lived in Canada in the area of Mt. Pleasant, Ontario. Freeman traveled to Kirtland to meet the Prophet Joseph Smith and asked if the Prophet would accompany him to Canada to teach to his sons. Joseph agreed to go. On October 5, 1833, Freeman, Joseph, and Sidney Rigdon left for Canada. The mission lasted about a month, traversed about five hundred miles, and resulted in the conversion of Freeman's two sons, their families, and several others.

This was only the beginning of Freeman and Huldah's service. Not long after the trip to Canada, Joseph Smith and Parley P. Pratt passed through on their way east to recruit volunteers for Zion's Camp. Not only did the fifty-five-year-old Freeman join, but so did two of his sons, Uriel and Levi.

Freeman was given a mission call by the Prophet to travel further east and raise more men and money for the march. Freeman, older than almost any other man in the company, completed that arduous journey. His family remembers the promises of the Prophet that their sacrifices were accepted of the Lord and that they had earned the martyr's crown.

Freeman and Huldah moved with the Saints from Kirtland to Missouri and from Missouri to Nauvoo—faithful and devoted all the while. Then in Nauvoo, Freeman was called on a mission to the eastern United States. In March 1842 in Boston, Massachusetts, Freeman advertised for a public meeting. Having heard of the persecution of the Latter-day Saints in Missouri, Abijah Tewkesbury attended that meeting, and due to the "magnetizing influence" of Freeman Nickerson, Abijah was converted, and the first branch of the Church in Boston was organized.

Freeman returned home to Nauvoo, and in the spring of 1844 was called out again to preach the gospel and campaign for Joseph Smith for President of the United States. He was on that mission when Joseph was martyred in June 1844.

In 1846, the Saints had fled Nauvoo and followed Brigham Young to the Rocky Mountains. By late summer, only the poorest remained behind in Nauvoo. Freeman's family was provisioned and prepared, but Freeman was on a mission to the East—his fourth extended mission. They could not leave without him. Mobs continually harassed and assaulted those remaining Saints, including Freeman's family.

In August, Freeman finally returned from his mission, but was so ill the family could not leave. Nauvoo became a city under siege as mobs attacked and drove the Saints out. On September 28, 1846, the Nickersons had no choice: sick or not, they loaded their wagon and trudged toward the river. As they passed down Parley Street, they looked back to see the mob ransack their home and then burn it to the ground. That night they crossed the river by the light of a burning city.

As the family continued westward, Freeman remained sick and could not regain his strength. He continued to weaken until finally on a cold January day under a makeshift shelter on the Chariton River in Iowa, Freeman Nickerson breathed his last.

A memorial plaque was placed to honor Freeman Nickerson in Chariton, Iowa. Part of the inscription reads, "He who has no feeling of veneration for his predecessors should expect none from those who follow him."

Sources: Andrew Jenson, *Latter-day Saint Biographical Encyclopedia* (1901), 1:690; *archive.org*

Freeman Nickerson, Missionary Database, *history.churchofjesuschrist.org*

Freeman Nickerson, the son of Eleazer Nickerson and Thankful Chase, was born February 5, 1779, at South Dennis, Barnstable County, Massachusetts. A seaman by trade, he married Huldah Chapman on January 19, 1801, at Cavendish. Freeman served as an officer in the Vermont infantry in the War of 1812. He was baptized a member of The Church of Jesus Christ of Latter-day Saints by Zerubbabel Snow in April 1833 near Dayton, and he was ordained a deacon by Edmund Fisher soon after. Freeman visited Joseph Smith in September 1833 at Kirtland, Geauga County, Ohio, and persuaded Joseph Smith and Sidney Rigdon to accompany him to Mount Pleasant, Brantford Township, Wentworth County, Gore District (later in Brant County, Ontario), Upper Canada, to proselytize among his children. Freeman served missions to the eastern United States and Canada in 1844 and 1846. He left Nauvoo for the West as part of the Latter-day Saint exodus in September 1846. He never reached the Salt Lake Valley, dying January 22, 1847, at Chariton River, Iowa.

Source: Freeman Nickerson, *josephsmithpapers.org*

Nora and John: She Married a Prophet

ora was born October 6, 1796, at Peel, on the Isle of Man. Her father was the captain of a slave-trading ship, the *Helen*. Nora, however, was given a proper upbringing and became refined and well-educated. When she was just fourteen, her father was killed at sea while putting down a mutiny. In order to help support her family, Nora left home to work.

In time, Nora joined the house of a Governor Smelt, governor of the Isle of Man. There she associated with many important people. Among them, she became good friends with a young woman who was married to the secretary of Lord Aylmer, the newly appointed governor of Canada. When the governor left for Canada, Nora's friend asked her to accompany them. At first Nora refused, but as she was wont to do with such serious matters, she prayed and asked the Lord to help her find answers in her Bible. While praying, she opened her Bible at random and read the following, "Get thee out of thy country, and from thy kindred and from thy father's house, into a land that I will shew thee" (Genesis 12:1).

With that, Nora became convinced that it was the will of God that she should make the voyage. In May 1832, she left for the New World.

Nora settled in Toronto, Canada. Once there she renewed her association with the Methodists, where she became acquainted with John, a young immigrant from England. John was a Methodist lay preacher and very devout. Both were seekers, and soon they became friends.

In time "John confided in Nora [a] revelation in his youth through which he knew he would preach the gospel in America, and it was a message of greater import and power than he then had."

As her class leader, John soon found himself attracted to the slender and dark-haired Nora, who, at thirty-six, was mature, accomplished, charming, witty, and possessed all the attainments of a lady of culture. It was B.H. Roberts who would further describe her as "refined both by nature and education, gentle and lady-like in manner, witty, intelligent, gifted with rare conversational powers, possessed of a deep religious sentiment, and, withal, remarkable for the beauty of her person."

John began to court Nora, but Nora wasn't interested. "She thought him handsome but unpolished; he hadn't been to the right schools nor attended a university; his intellectualism was flawed by gaps of the self-educated. Beneath the charm and humor crouched the tiger. He was a man who would always be involved in battles for principle. Would she want such a life?" She was not sure.

Notwithstanding her seeming reluctance, John proposed. She turned him down. There were other reasons for her coolness, not

146

the least of which was their age difference: Nora was thirty-six years old, and John was twenty-four. Nevertheless, John was persistent, asking the Almighty to intervene with Nora on his behalf.

Then Nora experienced a dream in which she saw herself as John's wife—and happy. She took it as a revelation from God. When John asked again, Nora accepted. They were married January 29, 1833.

Little could Nora—her full name Leonora—know that the man she married that day, John Taylor, would himself become every bit as much a prophet as those she loved in her Bible—a man renowned for his courage and intellect, who indeed would stand for principle like a tiger. For those principles he was wounded at Carthage in 1844 and died in exile for his faith in 1887.

Sources: Samuel W. Taylor, *The Kingdom or Nothing: The Life of John Taylor, Militant Mormon* (New York: MacMillan Publishing Co., 1976)

Ann Laemmlen Lewis, "John Taylor's Conversion in Toronto, Upper Canada, 1836," *online*

Craig K. Manscill, Dennis A. Wright, Robert C. Freeman, *Presidents of the Church: The Lives and Teachings of the Modern Prophets,* (Cedar Fort, Inc. 2008) chapter 3

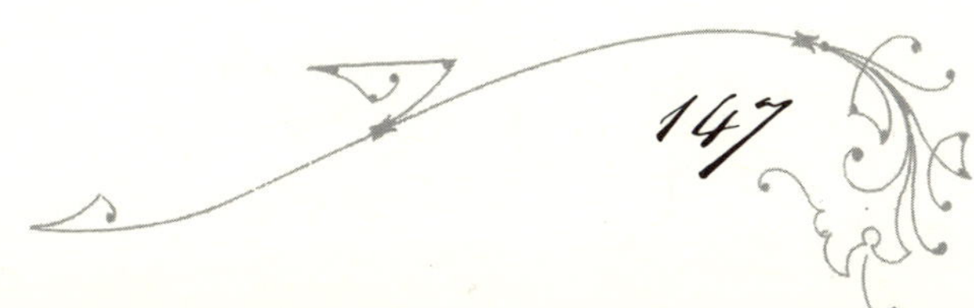

Leonora Cannon, the daughter of George Cannon and Leonora Callister, was born October 6, 1796, at Peel, Isle of Man. She immigrated to Canada in 1831 and married John Taylor in 1833; they had four children. Leonora was baptized a member of The Church of Jesus Christ of Latter-day Saints in Canada in 1836. From 1838 to 1846, she moved to Kirtland, Geauga County, Ohio; to Far West, Caldwell County, Missouri; to Quincy, Adams County, Illinois; to Montrose, Lee County, Iowa Territory; and to Nauvoo, Hancock County, Illinois. Leonora joined the Female Relief Society of Nauvoo as a founding member on March 17, 1842. She traveled to the Salt Lake Valley in 1847 and lived in the Salt Lake City Fourteenth Ward, where she participated in the Fourteenth Ward Relief Society. Leonora died December 9, 1868, at Salt Lake City.

Source: Leonora Cannon Taylor, *churchhistorianspress.org*

A Branch of Joseph's Calling

No sooner was the Book of Mormon off Grandin's press in Palmyra than Joseph was reassigned. The project to which he was assigned is little known and even less understood, even by Joseph's own people, yet it was so critical a work that he devoted much of his time to it for more than two years. The endeavor was launched as a commandment from the Almighty Himself and shepherded by Him to its completion. Joseph would later call this monumental work a "branch of his calling."

It was known and prophesied millennia before that Joseph would do this work. Moses himself looked forward to it. It was an integral component of the Restoration. So much of Joseph's doctrine—so many of the great revelations of the Restoration—came because of this effort.

The contribution of this work to the corpus of Latter-day Saint theology is incalculable. And that doesn't even include the ways in which it contributed to the personal education and edification of Joseph Smith himself.

Today many of us hold it in our hands, pack it off to Church, and seldom appreciate what we have. What is it? The Joseph Smith Translation of the Bible (JST).

As to what the JST is and its attendant power, the Lord told Joseph at the outset, "The scriptures shall be given even as they are in mine own bosom to the salvation of mine own elect" (D&C 35:20). How did it come to be? A scribe sat waiting with paper, pen, and ink. Joseph sat down with the large family Bible he purchased from E. B. Grandin and began to read under the influence of the Holy Ghost. As he read without the aid of seer stones or the Urim and Thummim, his mind was opened, inspired, and enlightened.

As Joseph read the text, he dictated changes. Sometimes there were no changes. Sometimes the changes were as minor as correcting punctuation, spelling, or grammar. Other times there were small deletions. Most impressively, sometimes whole chapters detailing intricate narratives of doctrine and history were revealed to Joseph, such as the writings about Enoch or Joseph of Egypt.

From the fountain of his expanded mind, Joseph dictated these new passages to his scribe, word for word, at a pace slow enough to be written long hand, without ever losing his train of thought, having to start over, or needing to gather his creativity.

Just the process as described by witnesses is miraculous considering the material revealed, but the miracle becomes utterly astonishing when the work is carefully studied and pondered. How could a twenty-four-year-old uneducated farmer from the frontier have produced such a work? It is inconceivable, making the JST another tangible testament with the Book of Mormon that Joseph Smith was an instrument of the Lord.

Many have opined that Joseph never finished it or that its text was adulterated after he died, but both ideas are false.

Perhaps its greatest contribution is its witness of the Savior. The JST reveals a greater Christ—more noble, and even more divine—making the JST another testament of Christ and the most correct of any Bible on earth.

Source: History of the Saints Interview with Kent L. Jackson, July 2014

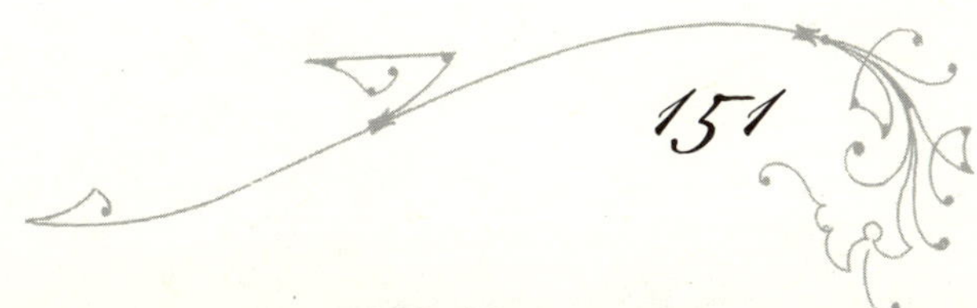

151

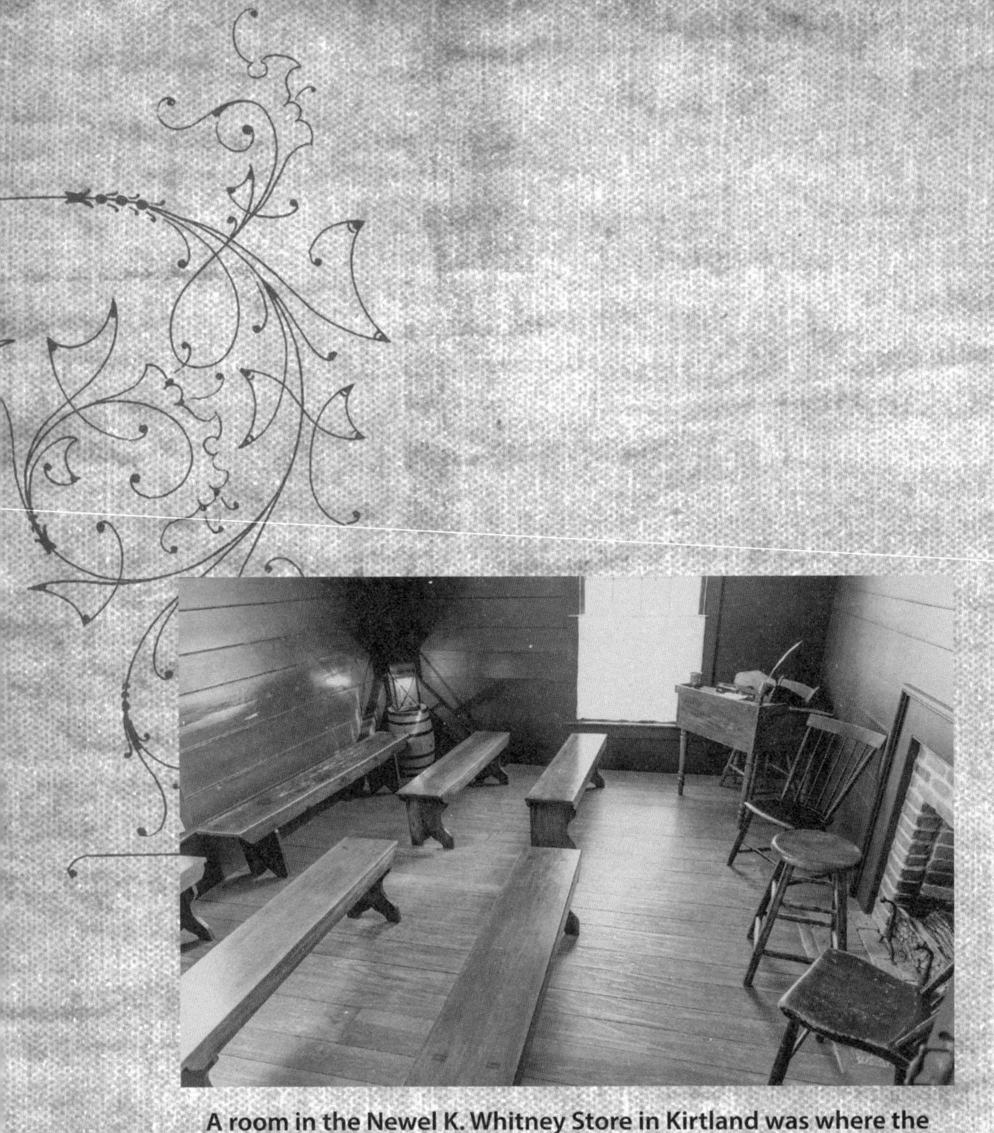

A room in the Newel K. Whitney Store in Kirtland was where the School of the Prophets met; photo by Robert E. Sorenson

The School of
the Prophets

Who could have known that out of such small beginnings would come forth such great things?

It began in December 1832. A revelation was received by the Prophet Joseph Smith that commanded, "I give unto you, who are the first laborers in this last kingdom, a commandment that you assemble yourselves together, and organize yourselves" (D&C 88:74). Accordingly, on January 22, 1833, the School of the Prophets was organized with fourteen charter members, among whom were Joseph and Hyrum Smith, Orson Hyde, Orson Pratt, and Levi W. Hancock.

For the next three months, these men met in a small room on the second floor of the Newel K. Whitney Store. They had been instructed by revelation to "teach one another the doctrine of the Kingdom" (D&C 88:77). Their curriculum was "of things both in heaven and in the earth; things which have been, things which are, things which must shortly come to pass, things which are at home, things which are abroad" (D&C 88:79). In short, they were to learn everything about everything, and why? The Lord said, "That

153

ye may be prepared in all things when I shall send you again to magnify the calling whereunto I have called you" (D&C 88:80).

The discipline expected of these men was extraordinary. They were to rise before dawn and come to school fasting and praying. They were to love one another and to cease from all laughter, light speeches, pride, and all wicked doings. They were to retire to their beds early and arise early, and above all else, they were to clothe themselves with charity. After a full day of fasting and instruction, they partook of sacramental bread and wine around four p.m., and the school closed for the day.

On February 27, 1833, another revelation was directed to those brethren—a revelation intended to purify them spiritually. We call it the Word of Wisdom.

On March 18, 1833, the Prophet Joseph boldly announced to the brethren that those sufficiently pure would see visions. On that day, sometime around noon, John Murdock described,

> The visions of my mind were opened, and the
> eyes of my understanding were enlightened and
> I saw the form of a man most lovely. The visage
> of his face was sound and fair as the sun. His hair
> a bright silver gray, curled in the most majestic
> form. His eyes a keen, penetrating blue, and the
> skin of his neck a most beautiful white. And he
> was covered from the neck to the feet with a loose
> garment, pure white, whiter than any garment I
> have ever before seen. His countenance was most

penetrating, and yet most lovely. And while I was
endeavoring to comprehend the whole personage from head to feet, it slipped from me and the
vision was closed up. But it left on my mind the
impression of love for months that I never felt
before to that degree.

To have experienced such things, and to have spent three
months learning at the feet of the Prophet Joseph—can you imagine?

This was the first official Church school—the beginnings of
the Church Educational System. For any of you who have attended
a seminary class, a Church school, Sunday school—or any class,
anywhere, sponsored by the Church—that little group of men
coming to school on those cold Kirtland mornings and the principles they espoused are a standard and an example to us all.

Source: History of the Saints Interviews with Alexander L. Baugh, January
2015, and Andrew M. Hedges, September 2014

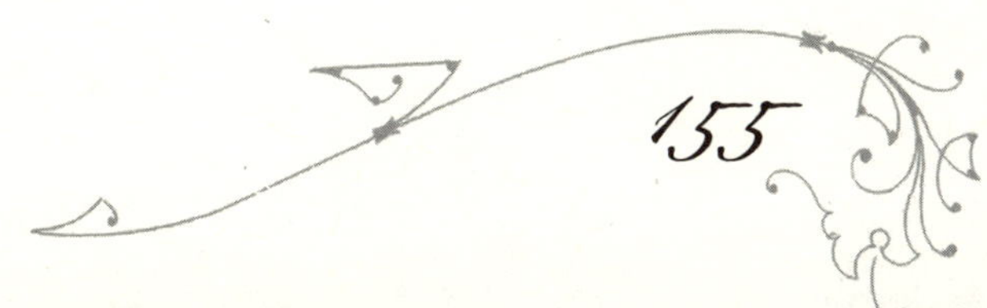

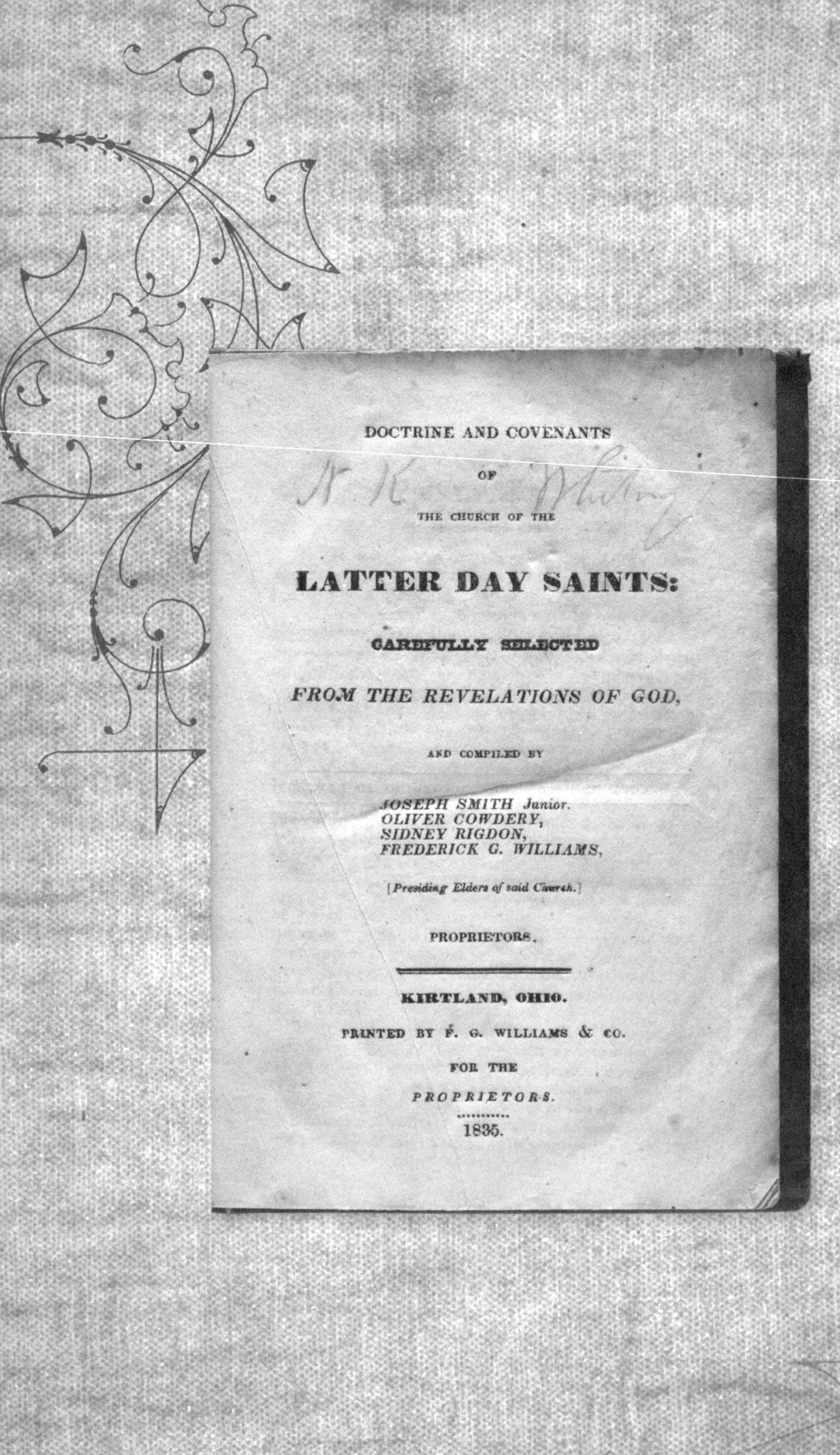

DOCTRINE AND COVENANTS

OF

THE CHURCH OF THE

LATTER DAY SAINTS:

CAREFULLY SELECTED

FROM THE REVELATIONS OF GOD,

AND COMPILED BY

JOSEPH SMITH Junior.
OLIVER COWDERY,
SIDNEY RIGDON,
FREDERICK G. WILLIAMS,

[*Presiding Elders of said Church.*]

PROPRIETORS.

KIRTLAND, OHIO.

PRINTED BY F. G. WILLIAMS & CO.

FOR THE

PROPRIETORS.

1835.

The Origins of the Doctrine and Covenants

On September 24, 1834, in Kirtland, Ohio, a council of fifteen men presided over by Joseph Smith met to consider the doctrine of Christ "for the government of the Church of Latter-Day Saints." A scripture publication committee was appointed consisting of the First Presidency, and theirs was no light task. It was concluded that the doctrines of Christ be assembled in this new volume from the Bible, Book of Mormon, "and the revelations which [had] been given to the church up to [that] date."

Less than one year later, on August 17, 1834, Oliver Cowdery arose with the newly published book in hand and called for a vote from the quorums of the Church assembled. In the course of that sustaining, certain leaders spoke and bore their witness of the book. Among them was President John Smith, the uncle of the Prophet Joseph. The minutes record that "President John Smith arose and testified his joy, that we have at length received the long wished for document to govern the church in righteousness and bring the Elders to see eye to eye." He then testified that the revelations "came from God." President Smith then called for the vote of his quorum, "that they would receive the Book as the rule of their faith and practice, and put themselves under the guidance of the same." The vote was unanimous.

And so it went through every quorum down to the deacons, until finally "a vote was called from the general assembly of the saints." The vote carried and the new book was received as scripture.

And thus was born the Doctrine and Covenants of The Church of Jesus Christ of Latter-day Saints. It received its unique name from the fact that the first seventy pages of the text were the Lectures on Faith that contained, it was reasoned, the doctrines of the Church. Following that were the revelations received by Joseph Smith that contained the covenants or commandments of God to the Saints of the last days—in short, it was the Doctrine and Covenants. It was and is that volume meant to govern the Church of Christ and bring us all to see eye to eye with the Almighty.

Sources: Doctrine and Covenants, 1835, 1; Minutes, 24 September 1834, 76; Minutes, 17 August 1835, 98, *josephsmithpapers.org*

The Prayer of the Lost

In the spring of 1834, young Jedediah Grant was traveling from Ohio to Missouri with a large group of men in a company called Zion's Camp. As the camp journeyed, Jedediah moved off away from them into the woods to hunt game. It wasn't long before he was ten or eleven miles from the moving body of men, and he had no idea in which direction they had gone.

"I entirely lost the track," he said, "and having no compass, I knew not towards what point I should travel. I kept traveling on till the afterpart of the day; I then concluded I would pray, but I could not get any impression where the camp was."

Jedediah persisted in prayer, and soon the Spirit of the Lord gave him an impression. He opened his eyes, and there before him was the camp moving on in regular order.

"I could see it just as clear as I did in the morning," he said, "there were the people, the wagons and horses, all in their places as I left them in the forepart of the day, and I supposed they were not more than 80 rods off."

But at that moment, Jedediah looked away, and when he looked back in the same direction the camp was gone. It was not there. He decided to travel in the direction he had seen the camp, and after covering another eight to ten miles he came upon them—looking exactly as he had seen them in vision.

Source: *Journal of Discourses,* Volume 3, Discourse 2

Jedediah M. Grant, the son of Joshua Grant and Athalia Howard, was born February 21, 1816, in Union, Broome County, New York. A farmer, he was baptized a member of The Church of Jesus Christ of Latter-day Saints by John F. Boynton on March 21, 1833. Jedediah participated in the Camp of Israel expedition to Missouri in 1834. He married Caroline Van Dyke on July 2, 1844, in Nauvoo. Jedediah was appointed captain of a company of emigrating Latter-day Saints and moved to Salt Lake City June–October 1847. Ordained an Apostle in 1854 in Salt Lake City, Jedediah served as second counselor to Brigham Young in the First Presidency from 1854 to 1856. He died December 1, 1856, in Salt Lake City.

Source: Jedediah Morgan Grant, *josephsmithpapers.org*

We Will See
Some Visions

The Savior once said that He was the "light which shineth in darkness and the darkness comprehendeth it not" (D&C 10:58). Among other things, that means we live in the presence of light and glory that we see and cannot comprehend. It is said that we live far below our spiritual privileges. That begs the question: What if we could pierce that veil over our eyes and really see?

In 1905, the aged general authority Zebedee Coltrin shared the following testimony in a meeting in Spanish Fork, Utah:

> April, 1834, [I] had just returned to Kirtland from serving a mission where I met the Prophet Joseph Smith. Joseph asked me if I would go with him to a Conference at New Portage, Ohio. I agreed to go and journeyed there with Joseph Smith, Sidney Rigdon, and Oliver Cowdery.
>
> The next day . . . , "Joseph seemed to have a far off look in his eyes, or was looking at a distance

and presently he, Joseph, stepped between Brothers Cowdery and me and taking us by the arm, said, "Let's take a walk." We went to a place where there was some beautiful grass and grapevines and swampbeech interlaced. President Joseph Smith then said, "Let us pray." We all three prayed in turn—Joseph, Oliver, and me. Brother Joseph then said, "Now brethren, we will see some visions."

Joseph lay down on the ground on his back and stretched out his arms and we lay on them. The heavens gradually opened, and we saw a golden throne, on a circular foundation, something like a light house, and on the throne were two aged personages, having white hair, and clothed in white garments. They were the two most beautiful and perfect specimens of mankind we ever saw. Joseph said, "They are our first parents, Adam and Eve." Adam was a large, broad-shouldered man, and Eve as a woman, was as large in proportion.

Sources: "Remarks of Zebedee Coltrin on Kirtland, Ohio, History of the Church," Minutes, Salt Lake City School of the Prophets, October 3, 1883, *www.boap.org*

New Portage Church Conference, *josephsmithpapers.org*

Zebedee Coltrin, the son of John Coltrin and Sarah Graham, was born September 7, 1804, at Ovid, Seneca County, New York. Zebedee married Julia Ann Jennings in October 1828 and was baptized a member of The Church of Jesus Christ of Latter-day Saints by Solomon Hancock on January 9, 1831, at Strongsville, Cuyahoga County, Ohio. He attended the organizational meeting of the School of the Prophets January 22–23, 1833, in Kirtland, and participated in the Camp of Israel expedition to Missouri in 1834. Zebedee was appointed a president of the First Quorum of the Seventy on February 28, 1835, at Kirtland. His wife died in 1841, and he married Mary Mott on February 5, 1843. Zebedee migrated to the Salt Lake Valley with Brigham Young's vanguard pioneer company in 1847. In 1852, he settled at Spanish Fork, Utah County, Utah Territory, where he died July 21, 1887.

Zebedee Coltrin, *josephsmithpapers.org*

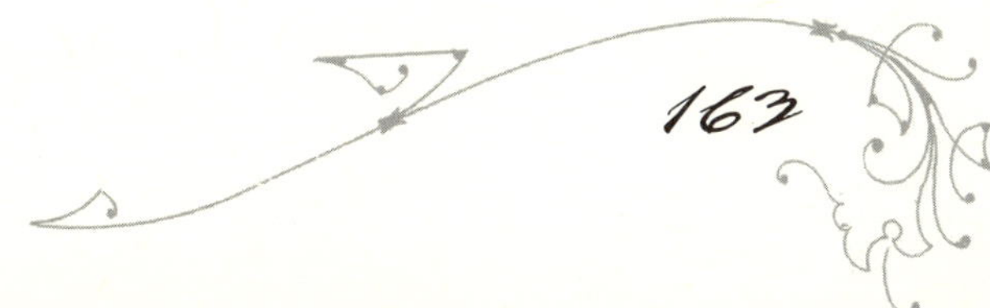

Temple at Kirtland, Ohio, dedicated March 27, 1836,
Library of Congress

"The Crowning of All the Prayers I Had Ever Heard"

In the fall of 1835, tensions arose between Joseph Smith and his younger brother, William. The tensions became so heated that William attempted to resign as an Apostle and went around Kirtland turning people against the Prophet.

On December 16, 1835, at a public debate at William's home in Kirtland, conflict between the two erupted and became increasingly heated until it became violent. According to Joseph's journal, as Joseph attempted to take off his coat, William attacked him and beat him to the point where he left the house "bruised and wounded." Joseph was "grieved beyond expression at the wickedness of his brother who Cain-like had sought to kill him."

It was during this tumultuous period that Daniel Tyler recorded this testimony.

At the time William Smith and others rebelled against the Prophet, as recorded in his history,

when the walls of the Kirtland Temple were raised but a few feet above the ground. I attended a meeting "on the flats," where "Joseph" presided.

Entering the schoolhouse a little before meeting opened, and gazing upon the man of God, I perceived sadness in his countenance and tears trickling down his cheeks. I naturally supposed the all-absorbing topic of the difficulty must be the cause. I was not mistaken. A few moments later a hymn was sung and he opened the meeting by prayer. Instead, however, of facing the audience, he turned his back and bowed upon his knees, facing the wall. This, I suppose, was done to hide his sorrow and tears.

I had heard men and women pray—especially the former—from the most ignorant, both as to letters and intellect, to the most learned and eloquent, but never until then had I heard a man address his Maker as though He was present listening as a kind father would listen to the sorrows of a dutiful child. Joseph was at that time unlearned, but that prayer, which was to a considerable extent in behalf of those who accused him of having gone astray and fallen into sin, that the Lord would forgive them and open their eyes that they might see aright— that prayer, I say, to my humble mind, partook of the learning and eloquence of heaven.

There was no ostentation, no raising of the voice as by enthusiasm, but a plain conversational tone, as a man would address a present friend. It appeared to me as though, in case the veil were taken away, I could see the Lord standing facing His humblest of all servants I had ever seen. Whether this was really the case I cannot say; but one thing I can say, it was the crowning, so to speak, of all the prayers I ever heard.

After the prayer another hymn was sung. When Joseph arose and addressed the congregation, he spoke of his many troubles, and said he often wondered why it was that he should have so much trouble in the house of his friends, and he wept as though his heart would break. Finally he said: "The Lord once told me that if at any time I got into deep trouble and could see no way out of it, if I would prophesy in His name, he would fulfill my words," and added: "I prophesy in the name of the Lord that those who have thought I was in transgression shall have a testimony this night that I am clear and stand approved before the Lord."

The next Sabbath his brother William and several others made humble confessions before the public. What their testimonies were, I never knew.

Sources: *Joseph Smith Papers, Documents,* Volume 5, 110–113

"Recollections of the Prophet Joseph Smith," *The Juvenile Instructor* 27 (1892)

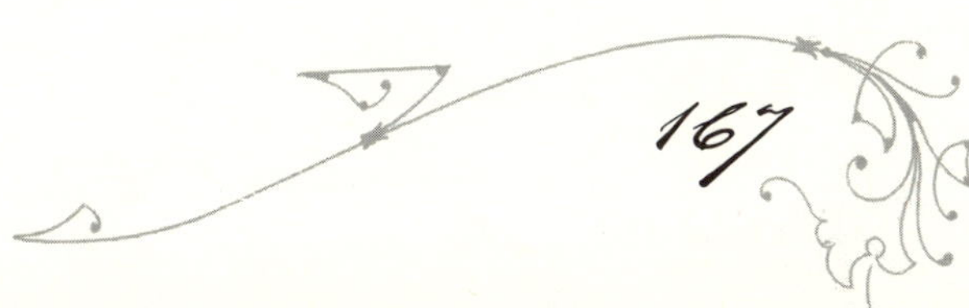

Lydia Goldthwaite

Newel and Lydia

Lydia Goldthwaite was born June 9, 1812, in Salem, Massachusetts, the third of twelve children in a loving family. In time her father moved the family to western New York. When she was sixteen, she met and married a charming, handsome fellow, Calvin Bailey, but he turned out to be an abusive drunk; her marriage subsequently became "the story of a man's cruelty and a woman's suffering."

In November 1830, Lydia gave birth to a little girl, Rosanna, who proved to be a blessing of comfort. Two years later she gave birth to a little boy she named Edwin. He lived only a day, and Lydia nearly died as well. In these awful circumstances, her husband announced he was moving. When Lydia told him she was too weak to travel, he abandoned her, leaving her utterly destitute.

Lydia moved home with her family. Then in January 1833, her little girl, Rosanna, died.

Lydia was distraught and inconsolable. Then a family friend, Eleazer Freeman Nickerson, invited her to come to Canada and live with him and his wife while she recovered. While there, Lydia met the Prophet Joseph Smith and heard him preach. She saw "his face become white and a shining glow seemed to beam from every feature."

With "trembling joy" Lydia was baptized on October 27, 1833. Two days later as Joseph was preparing to leave, he paced back and forth in deep thought. Finally, he spoke:

> Sister Lydia, great are your blessings. The Lord, your Savior, loves you, and will overrule all your past sorrows and afflictions for good unto you. Let your heart be comforted. . . . You shall yet be a savior to your father's house. Therefore be comforted, and let your heart rejoice, for the Lord has a great work for you to do. Be faithful and endure unto the end and all will be well.

In time Lydia joined the Saints in Kirtland. There she met Newel Knight, a widower. He "was tall, had light brown hair, a keen blue eye and a very energetic and determined manner." Love grew between them, but when Newel proposed marriage, Lydia tearfully declined.

Notwithstanding her husband's three-year absence, Lydia still considered herself married.

Distressed, Newel took the matter to Hyrum Smith. Hyrum

took it that very day to Joseph, and the Prophet said, "It is alright. She is his. The sooner they are married the better. Tell them no law shall hurt them. They need not fear either the law of God or man for it shall not touch them, and the Lord will bless them. This is the will of the Lord concerning the matter."

Upon hearing of the Prophet's pronouncement, Newel went immediately to Lydia. Filled with joy, Lydia threw herself on her knees and poured out her soul in thanks to God. Arrangements were made for the wedding the very next day. Hyrum mentioned he was going to invite a local justice of the peace to perform the ceremony, upon which Joseph said, "Stop, I will marry them myself."

On Tuesday, November 24, 1835, in Kirtland, Ohio, in a ceremony unique to him, the Prophet Joseph Smith married Newel Knight and Lydia Bailey. Lydia noted that once again as he spoke "that strange brilliant light shone through his features."

Not only were Lydia's past sorrows made up for in this happy union, but this was the first marriage ever performed by the Prophet Joseph Smith.

Time passed, and theirs was a happy, fulfilling union. Children came, and the family moved with the Saints from Kirtland to Missouri, then to Nauvoo, and finally on to the plains of Iowa as part of "the Mormon exodus."

At a place called Ponca Camp in northern Nebraska on Christmas day 1846, a fire swept down on the Saints, threatening to destroy all they had built. Newel and others fought the fire with all they had; by eleven that night they had managed to extinguish it, but at a terrible cost: Newel contracted pneumonia.

On January 1, 1847, Newel wrote in his journal the following,

I scarcely know why I am thus anxious, why
this world appears so trifling, or the things of this
world. I almost desire to leave this tenement of
clay, that my spirit may soar aloft and no longer
be held in bondage, yet my helpless family seem
to need my protection. For their sakes, and if I yet
have more to do on earth, or can do more good to
the living than to the dead, I am willing to remain
yet longer in the flesh. Thy will O Lord be done
and not mine.

On January 11, 1847, Lydia

. . . sat with tightly-closed hands and wild ago-
nized eyes watching the breath of the being she
loved better than life itself, slowly cease.

"Lydia," the dying voice faintly whispered,
"it is necessary for me to go. Joseph wants me. It
is needful that a messenger be sent with the true
condition of the Saints. Don't grieve too much, for
you will be protected."

"Oh Newel, don't speak so; don't give up; oh I
could not bear it. Think of me, Newel, here in an
Indian country alone, with seven little children.
No resting place for my feet, no one to counsel, to
guide, or to protect me. I cannot let you go."

The dying man looked at her a moment, and

then said with a peculiar look: "I will not leave
you now Lydia."

But he was in such terrible agony. When she could bear his suffering no longer, Lydia knelt and prayed that if it really was the will of the Lord, she would let him go. "The prayer was scarcely over ere a calm settled on the sufferer, and with one long loving look in the eyes of his beloved wife, the shadow lifted and the spirit fled."

That evening, Newel was buried. No lumber could be had, so Lydia had one of her wagon-boxes made into a crude coffin. The day was excessively cold, and some of the brethren had their fingers and feet frozen while digging the grave and performing the last offices of love for their honored captain and brother.

As Lydia looked out over the wilderness of snow and saw the men bearing away all that was left of her husband, it seemed that the flavor of life had fled and left only dregs—bitter, unavailing sorrow. But as she grew calmer, she whispered with poor, pale lips, "God rules."

Lydia joined the other Saints at Winter Quarters to prepare for the move west. As she attended the organization meeting, she felt overwhelmed at the enormity of it all. How could she make a one-thousand-mile journey into the wilderness with seven children? The burden weighed her very spirit down until she cried out in her pain, "Oh Newel, why hast thou left me!"

As she spoke those very words, Newel stood by her side, with a lovely smile on his face, and said:

Be calm, let not sorrow overcome you. It was
necessary that I should go. I was needed behind
the vail to represent the true condition of this
camp and people. You cannot fully comprehend it
now; but the time will come when you shall know
why I left you and our little ones. Therefore dry
up your tears. Be patient, I will go before you and
protect you in your journeyings. And you and
your little ones shall never perish for lack of food.

In time, Lydia and her children did make their way to Utah.
When the St. George Temple opened in 1877, Lydia was called to
be a temple worker, and she labored there for the rest of her days,
performing the sacred ordinances for hundreds of her kindred
dead, thus fulfilling the prophecy of Joseph that she would be a
savior to her people.

Sources: William G. Hartley, *Stand by My Servant Joseph: The Story of the Joseph Knight Family and the Restoration* (Salt Lake City: Deseret Book, 2003)

Jan Jansak Williams and LaRea Gibbons Strebe, "Lydia Knight: 'God Rules' Was Her Motto," *Ensign* (1977)

William G. Hartley, "Newel and Lydia Bailey Knight's Kirtland Love Story and Historic Wedding," *BYU Studies,* 39:4

Lydia Goldthwaite McClellan, *josephsmithpapers.org*

Susa Young Gates, *Lydia Knight's History: The First Book of the Noble Women's Lives* (1883), *archive.org*

Lydia Goldthwaite, the daughter of Jesse G. Goldthwaite and Sally Burt, was born June 9, 1812, at Sutton, Worcester County, Massachusetts. She married Calvin Bailey in the fall of 1828 but was deserted by him in 1832. Lydia moved to the home of Eleazer Freeman Nickerson at Mount Pleasant, Brantford Township, Wentworth County (later in Brant County), Gore District (later in Ontario), Upper Canada, in February 1833. A boardinghouse operator, weaver, and teacher, she was baptized a member of The Church of Jesus Christ of Latter-day Saints by Joseph Smith on October 27, 1833, at Mount Pleasant. She assisted Jerusha Smith, the wife of Hyrum Smith, in operating a boarding home in Kirtland in October 1835. She was married to Newel Knight by Joseph Smith on November 24, 1835, at Kirtland.

Lydia left Nauvoo as part of the Latter-day Saint exodus in 1846; she traveled with Newel Knight and others to Camp Ponca on Niobrara River in present-day Knox County, Nebraska, in 1846. Her husband Newel died in 1847. Lydia migrated to the Salt Lake Valley in 1850 and married James McClellan in 1864 in Payson. She was appointed to serve the St. George Temple. Her husband James died in 1880. Lydia moved to St. George, Washington County, Utah Territory, in 1880, where she died April 3, 1884.

Source: Lydia Goldthwaite McClellan, *josephsmithpapers.org*

Lorenzo Snow

"The Turning Point in My Life"

In September 1835, two men rode on horseback a distance of twenty-five miles from Mantua, Ohio, to the small community of Kirtland. One came from something of privileged background, his father being a prosperous farmer and a community leader. He had grown up with a close family and many opportunities for his day. He was at a time enrolled at the Presbyterian school of Oberlin College, where he was beginning a new semester of studies. The other man, considerably older, was a frontiersman born in Vermont and something of a rustic who had never had the privilege of learning, letters, and a life of opportunity. He had left home when just a boy and had carved out a homestead in the wilderness of southeastern Michigan. So removed was he from the joys of home and family life as a child that he lived out his days never knowing his own birth date.

As the two men rode along, they talked about many subjects. Years later, the young student said, "I was at first disposed to treat his opinions lightly, especially so, as they were not always clothed in grammatical language."

They talked first of philosophy, and then the subject turned to religion. In the course of conversation, the older man opened his scriptures and explained the plan of salvation and the conditions of the human family. As he did so, the disposition of his friend began to change. The young student found himself unable to resist the knowledge that this was a man of God.

"I felt pricked in my heart," he said. Though his language may not have been the most refined, the man "possessed a mind of deep thought and rich intelligence." He so opened the eyes and expanded the mind of the young man that it forever changed him.

Almost sixty-four years later, that student, now an old man himself at the end of his days, reflected on that day as follows:

> All the circumstances of my first and last meeting with [him] are as clear to my mind as if it were an occurrence of but yesterday. . . . He appeared to me then to be a remarkable man, and that impression has remained with me ever since. . . . This was the turning point in my life. What impressed me most was his absolute sincerity, his earnestness and his spiritual power.

During that original encounter, the older man bore a powerful witness of the truthfulness of the restored gospel and charged the young man to go before the Lord that night and ask for himself. The young man was true to that charge. He was subsequently baptized and went on to greatness in the eyes of the Almighty. That young man was Lorenzo Snow.

Lorenzo Snow never again had the opportunity of meeting with his friend in this life, for within three years his mentor died—

the first apostolic martyr of this dispensation, David W. Patten. In that encounter, Elder Patten demonstrated the undeniable power of simple, humble, fearless testimony.

Sources: Lycurgus A. Wilson, *Life of David W. Patten: The First Apostolic Martyr* (Early Church Reprints, 1983)

First Presidency General Letter, Salt Lake City, Utah, February 6, 1900

Lorenzo Snow, the son of Oliver Snow and Rosetta Leonora Pettibone, was born April 3, 1814, in Mantua, Portage County, Ohio. He attended Oberlin College and became a schoolteacher. Lorenzo was baptized a member of The Church of Jesus Christ of Latter-day Saints by John F. Boynton on June 19, 1836. He married in 1845 in Nauvoo. Lorenzo migrated to the Salt Lake Valley in 1848 and was ordained an Apostle on February 12, 1849. He served a mission to Italy in 1850–1852 and was appointed to serve a colonizing mission in what became Brigham City, Box Elder County, Utah, in 1853. Lorenzo served as president of the Quorum of the Twelve from 1889–1898. After the death of President Wilford Woodruff, Lorenzo presided over the Church from 1898–1901. He died October 10, 1901, in Salt Lake City; he is buried in Brigham City.

Source: Lorenzo Snow, *josephsmithpapers.org*

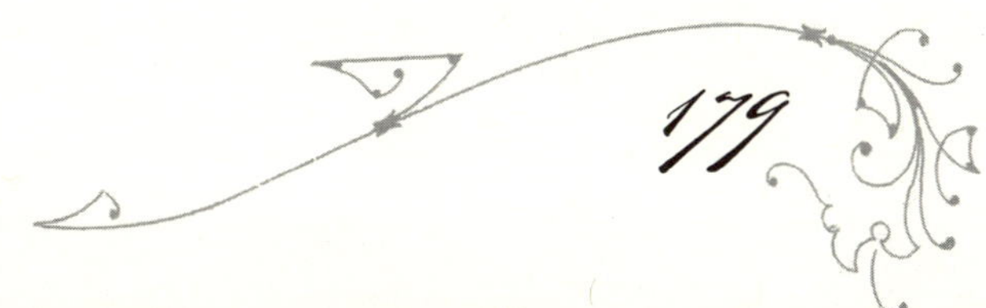

Joseph Smith's office, courtesy Val Brinkerhoff
and the Community of Christ

January 21, 1836—
A Night of Visions

On Thursday, January 21, 1836, sixteen men entered the Kirtland House of the Lord and climbed the winding staircase to the third-floor west office of Joseph Smith. They had washed and prepared themselves and were there to attend to the ordinance of sacred anointings as found in the Old Testament.

Joseph Smith Sr., being the oldest man present and the Patriarch of the Church, sat in the chair first. The First Presidency gathered around him, consecrated oil, and then anointed and blessed him, each in turn. Father Smith then rose and began to anoint those who had just blessed him. Then the members of the Presidency blessed each man following his anointing. Afterwards the other men in the room were similarly anointed and blessed.

On that significant night, the Spirit of the Lord was poured out in rich abundance. "The House was filled with the glory of God," and many received visions and the ministrations of angels, and so

testified. Among them was Joseph Smith Jr., who received one of the greatest and most comforting revelations ever given to man. He said:

> The Heavens were opened upon us and I beheld the Celestial Kingdom of God, and the glory thereof. . . . I saw the transcendent beauty of the gate through which the heirs of that kingdom will enter, which was like unto circling flames of fire; also the blazing throne of God, whereon was seated the Father and the Son. I saw the beautiful streets of that Kingdom which had the appearance of being paved with gold.

Joseph then described seeing several people, including his father and mother, who were both yet alive. Clearly, this was a vision of future events. But then Joseph saw his brother Alvin, who had died in 1823 at the age of twenty-five. How could Alvin be in the highest heaven with God, since he had never had the opportunity to be baptized?

With that question, Joseph was given the answer to one of the greatest theological questions of the millennia: What about all those who live and die without ever having the opportunity to hear the gospel and receive its ordinances? Are they saved or damned, and what is the justification for either? In answer to those questions, the Lord said, "All that shall die henceforth without a knowledge of it, who would have received it with all their hearts, shall be heirs of that kingdom. For I, the Lord, will judge all men

according to their works, according to the desire of their hearts"
(D&C 137:8–9).

Joseph then learned that all children who die before they
come of age are automatically saved in the highest heaven of God.
Can you imagine the joy just for Joseph, who had lost his beloved
brother Alvin and his own children to death? They were saved and
he would see them again!

But the remarkable visions did not stop there. Joseph also
saw into the terrestrial kingdom. He saw the Twelve Apostles and
the Savior in their midst in foreign lands. He saw those Apostles
escorted into the celestial kingdom of God, and many other things
that "the tongue of man cannot describe in full."

That night began a rich Pentecostal season lasting about fifteen weeks, a time during which Saints witnessed visions, angels,
spiritual gifts, and even the Savior Himself—more than perhaps at
any other time in history. Their experiences are written, recorded,
signed, and certified by eyewitnesses who were there.

Source: Visions, 21 January 1836 (D&C 137), 136, *josephsmithpapers.org*

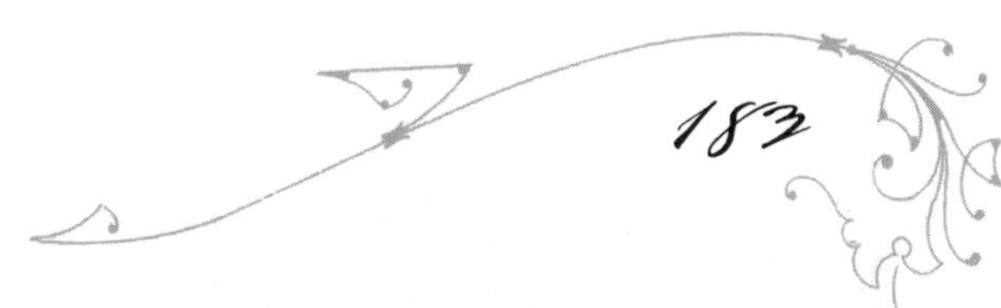

Elijah Restores the Power to Seal Families for Eternity,
by Gary E. Smith, courtesy
The Church of Jesus Christ of Latter-day Saints

A Remarkable
Easter Sunday
in Kirtland

On Easter Sunday morning, April 3, 1836, Joseph Smith and other members of the First Presidency opened the Kirtland House of the Lord and helped seat the congregation of about a thousand people. Those in attendance became attentive listeners as Thomas B. Marsh and David W. Patten preached from the stand.

That afternoon the congregation came again. Members of the Twelve blessed the emblems of the sacrament, and the Prophet Joseph Smith helped pass it. Then, according to witnesses, the veils were dropped in the large room dividing it into sections. Confirmations and the blessing of children were carried on in those gatherings as Joseph Smith and Oliver Cowdery climbed the pulpits at the west end of the building.

The pulpits themselves had been divided by veils according to tier. Joseph and Oliver ascended to the top tier, which was reserved for the First Presidency, and there knelt in silent prayer. Moments later, after Joseph and Oliver arose from prayer, the Lord Jesus Christ appeared to them in glory, accepting that House and promising that therein He would appear to His servants and speak to them. He further promised that many tens of thousands would rejoice over the blessings and endowments that had been and would be poured out in that house. Finally, He said, the sacred structure would become a monument famous the world over for what was revealed there.

The vision closed, and another vision burst upon them. Moses appeared and committed the keys of the gathering of Israel (see D&C 110:11). Then came Elias and "committed the dispensation of the gospel of Abraham, saying that in us and our seed all generations after us should be blessed" (D&C 110:12). And lastly, Elijah, the prophet holding the keys of the sealing power, appeared and committed his keys to them (see D&C 110:13–16).

It was no accident that Elijah appeared on that day. It was the season of the Passover, and Jews the world over had continued to set a place at the table for that prophet whose return had been prophesied for two millennia. Moreover, it was no coincidence that Jesus appeared on that day, it being 1,803 years to the very day of the Savior's Resurrection.

How often does Easter Sunday occur on both April 3 and 16 Nisan, as it did in AD 33? On average, it happens fewer than one time every century. The year 1836—the year the Saints gathered in the Kirtland Temple—was the only time that happened in the nineteenth century.

On that day, monumental and eternally orchestrated, all the keys of the priesthood necessary to gather the lost families of Israel, organize them once again into family units, and seal upon them the ordinances to exalt them were made fully operative. Unequivocally, individually, and collectively, it was the most important single day in human history since the Resurrection of Jesus Christ.

Sources: Journal, 1835–1836, 191, *www.josephsmithpapers.org*

John P. Pratt, "The Restoration of Priesthood Keys on Easter 1836, Part 2: Symbolism of Passover and of Elijah's Return," *Ensign,* (July 1985)

Parley P. Pratt

Is Anything Too Hard for the Lord?

When one young man was called to serve as a missionary in Toronto, Canada, he and a companion traveled into Canada via Niagara Falls, where they stopped and marveled at the wonders of God's hand in creation. The missionary arrived in Hamilton, Ontario, where he found a flourishing community, but he was bound for Toronto, on the other side of the lake.

The missionary faced a dilemma. Walking around the lake would take days and consist of an arduous journey. If he took passage across the lake, he would be there by day's end. But he had a problem: he was out of money. "Under these circumstances," he wrote, "I pondered what I should do. I had many times received answers to prayer in such matters, but now it seemed hard to exercise faith . . . because I was among strangers and entirely unknown."

How could the Lord possibly help him? No one in the town knew him. Nonetheless, at the Spirit's urging, the missionary retired to a secret place in the woods to pray for the money to make the boat journey across the lake.

Upon concluding his prayer, the missionary returned to Hamilton and began to talk to people. "I had not tarried many minutes," he said, "before I was accosted by a stranger who inquired my name and where I was going. He also asked me if I did not want some money."

When the missionary said that he did need money, the man gave him ten dollars and a letter of introduction to a man named Taylor in Toronto.

The missionary arrived in Toronto that night, called on the Taylors, and was put up for the night. The next morning, he traveled throughout the city seeking to establish contacts to begin his work, but no one would allow him to preach. None of the people would even open their houses to him. He had been promised great success in this city, yet he could not so much as open a conversation with anyone in town.

Once again the missionary retired to the woods and poured out his heart to God. "I had exhausted my influence and power without effect," he wrote. Upon finishing the prayer, he returned to the city and, having no other recourse, went to the Taylor home to collect his bag and be on his way.

Just then a woman named Isabella Walton entered the home. When the Taylors explained the missionary's presence, Isabella told the Taylors the following:

> Passing your door the Spirit bade me go in,
> but I said to myself, I will go in when I return;
> but the Spirit said unto me, 'go in now.' I accord-
> ingly came in and I am glad that I did so. Tell

the stranger he is welcome to my house. I am a
widow, but I have a spare room and bed, and food
in plenty. He shall have a home at my house and
a room to preach in just when he pleases. . . . I
feel by the Spirit that he is a man sent by the Lord
with a message which will do us good.

That very night, Isabella Walton took the missionary to her
home, invited all her friends and relatives to come over, and with
them listened attentively to the message. Like a sunrise over the
mountain, it was the opening of a miracle in Canada and subsequently in England. From that night forward, the work grew until
the missionary had to request help. Hundreds and finally thousands joined the Church because of that mission.

That praying missionary was Elder Parley P. Pratt. The year
was 1836, and among the significant converts made were Isabella
Walton; Joseph, Mary, and Mercy Fielding; and John and Leonora
Taylor. Indeed, nothing is too hard for the Lord, if we ask.

Source: Parley P. Pratt, *The Autobiography of Parley Parker Pratt,*
archive.org

Parley P. Pratt, the son of Jared Pratt and Charity Dickinson,
was born April 12, 1807, at Burlington, Otsego County, New York.
A farmer, editor, publisher, teacher, school administrator, legis-
lator, explorer, and author, he lived in Ohio 1826–1827. Parley

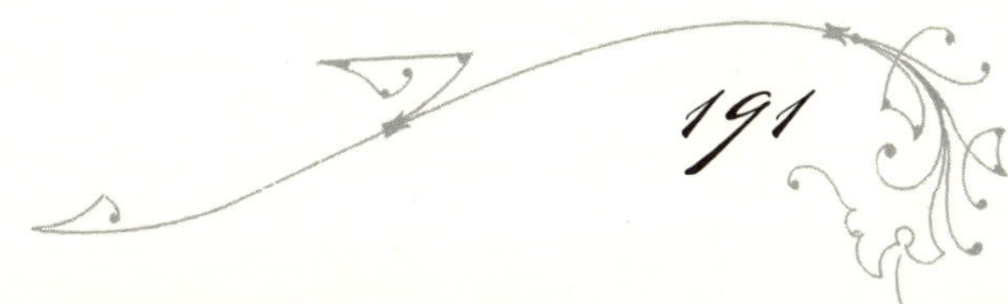

married Thankful Halsey on September 9, 1827, at Canaan, Columbia County, New York. He was baptized a member of The Church of Jesus Christ of Latter-day Saints and ordained an elder by Oliver Cowdery on September 1, 1830, at Seneca Lake, Seneca County, New York. Parley served a mission to unorganized Indian Territory and Missouri with Oliver Cowdery and others in 1830–1831; en route, they stopped at Kirtland, Geauga County, Ohio, and vicinity, where missionaries baptized some 130 people. He was ordained a member of the Quorum of the Twelve by Joseph Smith, David Whitmer, and Oliver Cowdery on February 21, 1835, and he served a mission to Canada from April to June 1836.

His wife Thankful died on March 25, 1837, and Parley married Mary Ann Frost Stearns on May 14, 1837, at Kirtland. He was jailed at Richmond, Ray County, and Columbia, Boone County, Missouri, in 1838–1839. Upon his release, Parley served a mission to England from 1839–1842. He was the first editor of *Latter-day Saints' Millennial Star*, published in Manchester, Lancashire, England, May 27, 1840. Parley participated in plural marriage during Joseph Smith's lifetime. Parley arrived in the Salt Lake Valley on September 28, 1847, and he led an exploration party into southern Utah Territory from November 1849 to February 1850. Parley was murdered May 13, 1857, at Van Buren, Crawford County, Arkansas.

Source: Parley Parker Pratt, *josephsmithpapers.org*

The Duty of Prayer

Years ago, there was a young college student who struggled with his testimony.

Through the powerful influence of others, his heart was touched, and he was convinced of the truthfulness of the gospel—*convinced* but not *converted*. He did not yet know for himself by the witness of the Spirit that it was true. But acting on faith, he went forward and was baptized. For many days after that, he prayed, he studied, and he yearned, but still there was no witness as the Savior promised in the Gospel of John.

Late one afternoon while busily engaged in his studies, the student became discouraged that he had not yet received an answer to his many prayers. The mood he was in became so oppressive that he couldn't study or concentrate, so he went outside and wandered through the forests and fields near his home. When the gloom of his mood only darkened, he finally realized he needed to pray.

The student had started a habit of going outside at a certain time and place each day for private prayer. But on this day, "the heavens,"

he said, "seemed like brass over my head." One voice inside whispered that he should pray; the other voice enticed him away from his prayers. He did not feel like going to his grove to pray.

Finally, after some struggle (or wrestle, if you will), the young student decided to keep his appointment with Heavenly Father. He knelt. No sooner had he opened his mouth than he heard something that resembled the rustling of silken robes over his head. Suddenly the Spirit of God descended upon him from head to foot, filling him with an indescribable witness and joy. All darkness and doubt were gone in an instant, and he knew that Jesus Christ is the Son of God and that the gospel is true.

"I knew," he later said, "that God had conferred on me that which is of greater value than all the wealth and honors worlds can bestow."

From that day to the day of his death he was true, giving his life to the witness he had gained—and what a life it was, filled with obedience, sacrifices, and miracles. Lorenzo Snow, that young college student, became a mighty man of God, all because of a day when he prayed because he was *supposed* to, not because he *wanted* to.

Source: "Chapter 3: Lifelong Conversion: Continuing to Advance in the Principles of Truth," *Teachings of Presidents of the Church: Lorenzo Snow,* Chapter 3 (2012)

Chatburn and Downham

In 1837, Heber C. Kimball, Orson Hyde, Joseph Fielding, and others were called to labor as missionaries in the British Isles; they centered their labors in Preston, England. In September of that year, Heber and Joseph ventured out into the countryside where Heber declared his intention of visiting Chatburn and Downham, two small villages northeast of Preston. "Several brethren endeavored to dissuade me from going," Heber said, "informing me there could be no prospect of success whatever as they had resisted all efforts for the last thirty years. I was informed they were wicked places."

Heber went anyway, telling the naysayers that "it was my business not to call the righteous but sinners to repentance."

Heber recorded what happened when they arrived in Chatburn:

> I was cordially received by the inhabitants
> who turned out in great numbers to hear me
> preach. They placed a barrel in the center of a

large barn for me to preach on. I preached to
them the first principles of the gospel, and a little
on the subject of the resurrection. When I concluded, I felt someone pulling at my coat, exclaim-
ing, "Maister, maister. Please sir, will you baptize
me?" "And me?" "And me?" exclaimed more than
a dozen voices. Accordingly, I went down into
the water and baptized twenty-five. I was engaged
with them until after midnight.

The next morning I returned to Downham and
baptized between 25 and 30 in the course of the
day. The next evening I returned to Chatburn. The
congregation was so numerous that I had to preach
in the open air, and stand on a stone wall, and afterwards baptized several. We were absent from Preston five days during which time Brother Fielding
and I baptized and confirmed about 110 persons.

Elder Fielding said of these experiences, "There is wonderful
work in Downham and Chatburn, two small villages. It appears as
though the whole of the inhabitants were turning to the Lord from
10 to 90 years old. It is truly affecting to see them."

On a subsequent visit to the area, Elder Kimball recalled:

I cannot refrain from relating an occur-
rence which took place while brother Fielding
and myself were passing through the village of
Chatburn on our way to Downham. Having been

observed approaching the village, news ran from
house to house, and immediately the noise of
their looms was hushed, and the people flocked to
their doors to welcome us and see us pass. More
than forty young people of the place ran to meet
us; some took hold of us and then of each other's
hands; several having hold of hands went before
us singing the songs of Zion, while their parents
gazed upon the scene with delight, and poured
their blessings upon our head and praised God
for sending us. The children continued with us to
Downham, a mile distant. Such a scene and such
gratitude I never witnessed before. And this from
those whose hearts were deemed too hard to be
penetrated by the gospel.

The brethren were thronged so much that they could scarcely
pass along the street. Heber continued:

On the morning when I left Chatburn many
were in tears thinking they should see my face no
more. When I left them my feelings were such as
I cannot describe. As I walked down the street, I
was followed by numbers; the doors were crowded
by the inmates of the houses to bid me farewell,
who could only give vent to their grief in sobs and
broken accents.

197

While contemplating this scene I was constrained to take off my hat, for I felt as if that place was holy ground. The spirit of the Lord rested down upon me and I was constrained to bless that whole region of country. We could hardly separate. My heart was like unto theirs and I thought my head was a fountain of tears, for I wept for several miles after I bid them adieu. I had to leave the road three times to go to streams of water to bathe my eyes.

When Heber returned home, he related his experience in Chatburn and Downham to the Prophet Joseph Smith, who explained, "Did you not understand it? That is a place where some of the old prophets travelled and dedicated that land, and their blessing fell upon you."

Is it possible that those people were remnants of the lost tribes of Israel? And is it possible that Jesus's Apostles visited there? There is so much of history yet to be revealed.

Sources: Journals of Heber C. Kimball

Peter Fagg, "The Conversion of Chatburn and Downham," *Meridian Magazine,* June 27, 2016

Index

Downham, England, missionary
    work in, 196–198

E

Easter
    occurring on same day as
    Passover, 186–187

    visions on in Kirtland Temple,
    185–187

Elias, appearance in Kirtland
    Temple, 186

Elijah
    appearance in Kirtland
    Temple, 186

    restored power to seal
    families, 184

Emma and Joseph Smith
    courtship of, 28

    differences in background,
    28–29

    marriage of, 29

Enoch, built first city of Zion,
    109–110

Ether, prophecy of about the new
    Jerusalem, 109

Eve and Adam, Joseph Smith Jr.
    vision of, 161–162

Evil spirit, possessing men at
    Church conference, 114

F

Fielding, Joseph
    conversion of, 191

mission to British Isles,
    195–198

Fielding, Mary
    conversion of, 191

Fielding, Mercy
    conversion of, 191

First Vision, 17–20
    painting depicting, 19

G

Gilbert and Whitney Store,
    destroyed by mob, 134

Glory, three degrees of, vision
    concerning, 130–131

Gold plates
    lithograph of Joseph obtain-
    ing, 38

    obedience key to obtaining,
    25

    unearthed at Cumorah, 23–26

Goldthwaite, Lydia
    baptism and blessing of, 170

    biographical details, 175

    birth of children with Calvin
    Bailey, 169

    death of children, 169

    image of, 168

    marriage to Calvin Bailey, 169

    marriage to Newel Knight,
    170–171

    meeting Joseph Smith Jr., 170

    reflections on husband's
    death, 172–173

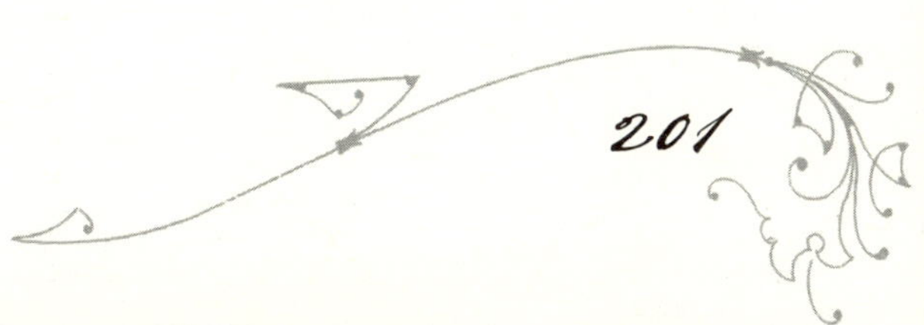